POWERLESS TO POWERFUL

Mark Mascolo

Table of Contents

Phase 3

Letter To The Reader

Welcome To Powerless To Powerful.

I call this The Great Awakening Of The Masculine Soul.

It is written for men. The guys out there battling for the rewards we all want out of life.

It's written for men in recovery. The guys out there coming back from the hell that is life in active addiction.

But it's also for women who are looking to understand men better.

In recovery we talk about experience, strength and hope.

My experience is:

As a man, I have been right where many of you have been. I have been the victor and I have been the victim. I have had it and I have had it not.

I have been the ultimate poser. Hiding behind careers and titles and stuff. I have hidden my addictions and hidden behind my addictions.

I had created a man I didn't even like. My definition of ego became; trying to get you to believe things about me, I didn't even like about myself.

I know what it's like to have distanced myself from God to the point I'm sure I have experienced hell.

Not only have I realized I was losing the battle, but I realized I was fighting for the wrong things.

As a man in recovery, I know what it's like to be terrified.

When I began my journey on the positive side of addiction in 1999, I had heard the statistics. The percentages of failure vs. success terrified me. I knew this was life or death for me. I loved my kids and my family, and I didn't want to die.

I've gotten a lot of it wrong. I've been through a divorce and a bankruptcy in recovery. I have gained things and lost things. I have watched people come and go. But, I have remained abstinent from my addictions while learning the difference between what is true and what is false, what is real and what is not.

My strength comes from the place that:

I spent the first 35 years of my life complicating everything.

I have spent the last 19 years uncomplicating it.

I erased the space created by my addictions between me and God and now understand more every day, that when I live my life with a purpose, I will raise my awareness to new possibilities and will realize the unlimited potential I have to make those possibilities a reality.

I had an experience in my first year of my recovery that changed everything for me. I found the information that my soul was longing for. It wasn't about the disease of addiction. It wasn't about the everyday struggles that men know as husbands, fathers and businessmen.

It was information that lit a fire in me and awakened a passion for life that I never knew existed.

What you are going to experience with this book is different. It is written in the exact opposite sequence most books are written in. I created the audio version first. The book was then transcribed from the recordings.

Why you ask?

Whether you are reading this or listening to the audio version, I want you to feel as if, it's sunset and we are having a relaxed conversation in front of a firepit. I don't want you to feel like I am talking at you.

I want to you to hear the information, but more importantly, feel the information.

<u>My hope is this</u>:

If you are looking for something you haven't found yet, no matter where you are on your journey, that this information will raise your awareness to a new level of thinking, awaken a fire that burns in the depths of your masculine soul and have you realize, "Yeah, This Is The Way I Really Want To Think Too".

Enjoy your journey through The Great Awakening.

We Have Also Created Some Powerful Online Resources At; PowerlessToPowerfulTheBook.com

Until We Meet, Be Powerful In All You Do!
God blesses,

Mark Mascolo

Tin Cup Farms, Clifton, Tennessee

There are so many people that I am grateful for what they have meant to the message in this book.

- To the God of my understanding, who is also the God beyond my understanding for defining a purpose for me, for raising my awareness to new possibilities and awakening the unlimited potential you instilled in my passionate masculine soul.

- To my 3 children, Marki, Michael and Tate. For always reminding me of what is good and right in this world. You make God's greatest gift and biggest responsibility, the gift of fatherhood, the driving force behind striving to become the man God calls me to be.

- To Theresa. Thank you for being strong enough to say the words that saved my life; "Get out of here until you get some help".

- To John. For being the guy that led me to the message.

- To Cumberland Heights. For your continued commitment to changing the world through addiction treatment.

- To my counselor James, for helping me see the man I aspired to be, needed a pivot point. RIP, sir, you were an effective helper of mankind.

- To Finney, Guy, Mary Ann, Johnny and Peggy, thank you.

- To the men in my aftercare group, your wisdom and guidance has been and continues to be immeasurable.

- To the members of 12 step recovery groups, thank you for being there.

- To my dad. Thank you for believing in me when you didn't know why. When your journey was over, the world lost one of God's kindest sons. RIP Pop.

- To my mom. All I can say is Thank You for always being my biggest cheerleader. God blessed me with you.

- To Ashley. My life changed forever when God led you into it. You make me better in everything I do and strive to do and to become. The message you continuously give me for loving me for who I am, and most importantly, who I challenge myself to become is the message that led me to God's purpose for me and for us. Thank you, my Angel.

Much love to you all.

I) Our Masculine Soul

What should I know about my masculine soul?

Every man born into this world has been given a great gift. This great gift costs us nothing, but its value is everything. It is given to us by Our Creator in an instant, but it can only be recognized over a lifetime. The gift is surrounded by mystery. Some men understand it, most do not. Some women understand it, most do not.

You ask, "What is this great and mysterious gift?"

On the 5th day God said, "Let us make mankind in our image, in our likeness....". So, God created mankind in his own image, in the image of God, He created them, and God blessed them.

On Days 1-4, God had created everything else, all the mountains and the oceans, the sun, the moon, the stars, the raging rivers, the forests, the waterfalls and all of the living creatures, all of the wild beauty that man was born into.

But something happened on that 5th day; The masculine soul was created in the image and likeness of The Creator. Look at all the power it took to create all of that. Mountains, oceans, all the wild animals and creatures.... and your masculine soul, in the image and likeness of God.

Now God created man and woman, not just 'people'. The masculine soul of a man is his, unique to him, a great gift he will spend a lifetime understanding. If stirring in your soul is a little wildness, men be grateful. If stirring in your soul is a desire for adventure, men be grateful. If stirring in your soul is a competitive nature that manifests itself in many ways (both positively and negatively), men be grateful. If stirring in your soul is a power that confuses you, men be grateful. That is the world God created for you to live in. Look at all the power, the wildness, the adventure He created for you to experience. It was not just then, it is now as well.

Day 6, God created all the vegetation, seed-bearing plants and trees.

Day 7 He rested.

II) The Story of Adam Is The Story of Every Man

How does the story of Adam affect me?

God formed a man from the dust of the ground and breathed into him the breath of life. His name was Adam. The name 'Adam' comes from a Hebrew word, 'adama' which means 'soil / earth'. God gave Adam everything. The land to care for, the animals, the vegetation and yes, God created woman. Why? Because He said, "It is not good for man to be alone". Adam was given everything he ever needed or desired and God said, "It's all yours just stay away from that tree. You can have all of this, just don't touch, 'THAT'". Adam was naked. This was the real Adam with a powerful self-image because he was born into all this abundance in the image and likeness of his Creator. Does naked mean physically naked or just void of any negative self-image? The real man, the man God created, Adam.

But, what did he do? You're right, he screwed it up. Instead of protecting her, she made a bad decision and he said, "Yeah, sounds good, I'll do it too".

You know the story, God comes back and says, "Adam, where are you?".

Adam says, "I'm over here, hiding behind this tree".

God says, "What are you doing over there hiding behind that tree? All the good stuff is out here."

Adam's answer.... "I'm naked".

Welcome to guilt, shame, negative self-image and negative self-worth. Adam felt awful, but when asked, "Why?", what did he do? He throws Eve under the bus and says, "She made me do it!". Welcome to blame and lack of personal responsibility.

So, why the bible lesson? Surely you didn't need to come here for that, right?

Well, here's the deal. The story of Adam is the story of every man. It is the story of me, it is the story of my dad, my sons, and it's the story of you. Every single day, God invites us into abundance. He is willing to give us, just like Adam, everything. Every day God comes into our lives and says, "Where are you, and why are you hiding?". And my answer, more times than not is, "I'm over here behind these trees and I'm naked.". Does naked mean physically naked? Hardly. Are the trees really physical trees I am hiding behind? Hardly. My nakedness is my feeling of inadequacy, negative self-image and negative self-worth. I can label the trees I am hiding behind as any number of things from my ego to my addictions. I can even hide my nakedness behind some of the good things in my life.

God isn't going to drag me kicking and screaming out from behind the trees. With my masculine soul, He gave me a free will, a gift of choice. The choices I make are up to me. So, God simply invites me. He says, "It's ok for you to stay over there, hiding. But, I'm just going to tell you, all the good stuff is out here!"

What God wants from me is to accept His invitation, but I can only do that if I am willing to put aside my nakedness and let the world see the real me. All my successes, all my failures, all my power and all my shortcomings. God created me, just like He created you.... unique. There has never been or will ever be another man born who is exactly like you. Our goal then becomes, to search for the real me, the real masculine heart and soul created in the image and likeness of God, Himself.

III) Addiction Creates Separation

Why do I feel like God quit believing in me?

The great gift was given to us at birth. We were born into this world, unique and perfect for who we are. Remember, in the image and likeness of our Creator. But what happens? We grow older and more experienced in the ways of the world. And many times, the ways of the world lead me away from the real me. You see, as a man, I am always looking for validation. I'm built that way. Competitive. I want to win. The validation I long for is, that I have what it takes to be a real man, the man I want you to see, not the man I was created to be.

My definition of ego is; the things I want you to see that I don't even like about myself. As men we all look for validation in everything we do. We look for it in the women we date, in our careers, in the stuff we have and even in the accomplishments of our kids. This validation is a 'look at me, look at me, I've got what it takes' that many times covers up our nakedness, our feelings of inadequacy, our negative self-image.

Enter addiction. Addiction has many faces. Alcohol, legal and illegal drugs, gambling, pornography, sex, work, and the list goes on and on. When I talk about hiding behind the trees labeled 'ego' and 'my addictions', this is what I am referring to. Every man, no matter how great he looks on the surface, has a chink in his armor. An Achilles Heel, that given the right circumstances and sequence can reveal itself in all kinds of chaos and disaster. Many times, our addiction shows up as harmless fun to begin with, becomes one of the trees to hide our nakedness and in the end becomes a life and death struggle fought deep inside our masculine soul.

I know in my addiction, I asked many times, "God, where are you?". I was convinced that He had either quit listening or abandoned me altogether. How could I expect God to stick around and continue to believe an addict like me? But what I now realize, is that God never left. My addictions created the separation. My thoughts and actions created my results. Addictive thoughts, addictive actions create the results of an addict. It is insane to think it could be any other way. God never left. I did. The separation was because of me, not because of Him.

IV) The Surrender and The Battle

Who am I in a battle with?

In our society, true masculinity is under attack. Whoa, wait. It is not actually true masculinity that is being attacked, it is false masculinity that seems to be the blanket thrown over all masculinity. Yes, that is correct, there is a true masculinity and a false masculinity. Again, some men understand it, most do not. Some women understand it, most do not.

Masculinity is abused by the ignorant and the knowledgeable. It is used as a weapon by our politicians and the press. False masculinity is everywhere. It is in the egos of professional athletes and entertainers. It is in the force men use for gain in personal and professional relationships. It is falsely portrayed success as it lures men of all ages from young boys, teenagers and adults. We see it every day in advertising. We see it as it manifests itself in some ways that may seem harmless and other ways that are absolutely horrific. False masculinity is a force for evil. False masculinity is my ego, it is my addictions, it is what I must surrender. False masculinity separates me from God. This surrender, the surrender of my addictions begins to erase my separation from God.

True masculinity is of God. It is the image and the likeness you were created in. True masculinity creates real power. True masculinity helps a man find his purpose, become aware of an abundance of new possibilities and most importantly, it awakens the masculine soul to the unlimited potential given to you in the image and likeness of, and by your Creator.

V) Our True Identity

Where do I find the real me?

My name is Mark, and I am an addict. When you hear that, how does that make you feel? What does it mean? There are all the negative thoughts; alcohol, drugs, pornography, work, and on and on. To many it would mean that I am identified by my problems, by my weaknesses, by my powerlessness. To many who repeat it, it can bring with it a negative self-image and a negative self-worth.

We all go through life with labels that are like words written on the back of a t-shirt, proclaiming who we are and what we are. These labels could be the identity labels we give ourselves or the ones we accept that are given us by others or a group. These labels can be negative. If you had to put a label on a t-shirt about how you feel about yourself, would it be one that disempowers you? The negative ones can almost be the easier ones to wear, right? Addicted, broke, divorced, bankrupt, hopeless, bad in relationships, struggling, just to name a few.

Or, by contrast, addicted, great dad, awesome husband, passionate, purposeful and powerful. "But, Mark, you put addicted in there in both negative and positive". Correct! It is not a typo for those of you reading and not something I said in error. My name is Mark, and I am an addict. I am addicted to a great relationship with a woman I love. I am addicted to being a father. I am addicted to spending time in the outdoors with people I love and care about. I am addicted to the powerful purpose God has for my life. I am addicted to helping others see that they too are powerful. I am addicted to my spiritual connection with a God of my understanding and the same God who is beyond my understanding. There was once a time when I was addicted to the negative. Today, I didn't change the fact that I am an addict, I just changed addictions.

My negative addictions were going to kill me. Being addicted to the positive motivates, inspires and empowers me.

I am a firm believer, God wants me and you to step into the abundance He has for us. A man's #1 purpose is to discover his #1 purpose. The purpose can only become a reality when he, me and you, step out from behind the trees we hide behind, in all our nakedness and allow the world to see the powerful image and likeness of The One who created us. God longs for us to not be a spectator in the game of life. He wants us, invites us, to be an active participant in creating our life with Him. Not just identifying ourselves with our shortcomings but accepting and identifying our true selves as powerful examples of not just God-given, but God-applied potential.

VI) The 3 Phases of Recovery

I never heard about The 3 Phases of recovery, what are they?

3 Phases of Recovery
- The first phase is The Sustained Physical Abstinence Phase
- The second phase is The Rebuilding Phase
- The third phase is The Discovery and Life's Purpose Phase

Phase 1 Sustained Physical Abstinence:
This is the physical, just quit using, phase. "Don't use and go to meetings!" is the message for Phase 1 Recovery. It feels good to be around people who are all fighting the same problem. Guidance from a group or a sponsor and the power of social proof, just being around people who all have a common cause, is the power in Phase 1. This is the addition by subtraction phase. We feel better for removing the source of so much pain. Some people choose to stay in Phase 1 and settle for 'just not miserable' as good enough, and there is absolutely nothing wrong with that.

Phase 2 Rebuilding:
In the second phase, we learn how to change self-defeating behaviors and begin the rebuilding of the life that crumbled because of our addiction. Successful relationships in recovery help us with successful relationships outside of the confines of recovery. Service work, learning to forgive and how to be forgiven are instrumental in Phase 2. We are introduced to the concept that there just may be more to this than 'just not using'.

 "Go apply the principles you learned at the meetings into your everyday life!" is the message of real recovery in Phase 2. Anyone can be a spiritual giant sitting behind closed doors at a meeting. How do you treat a person in traffic or the person taking too much time at the cash register? How do you treat your parents, your kids, your spouse or partner? What's the language you use to yourself? Is it empowering, or disempowering?

Phase 3 Discovery and Life's Purpose:

Most are unaware this phase even exists. Painting the picture of your ideal life is the core of Phase 3. This is where flourishing in recovery leads to flourishing in life. We simply can't afford to hold on to the, 'us against the world' mentality. Phase 3 reveals hidden strengths and gives life meaning. It's the place where we learn to reach for a life we are truly happy with, not just one we are choosing to settle for. What many people find is the source of their addiction was the misuse of a creative force inside them. The language of Phase 3 is to learn how to celebrate positive addictions. This is the language you probably won't hear at meetings and your sponsor probably has no clue about either. This is the language of what Powerless To Powerful, The Great Awakening of The Masculine Soul is all about. It requires an extreme level of trust and it's not for the timid.

The first thing to remember here is that all 3 Phases of Recovery are inclusive of the previous phase. And this is where the majority of stumbling blocks occur.

The first major stumbling block is trying to rebuild the life that crumbled (Phase 2) before a period of sustained abstinence (Phase 1). Few people have been successful rebuilding their life without sustained (not brief, not intermittent) abstinence.

The second stumbling block seems to be unrest and boredom. We have reached a place where, removed from the pain, we seem to forget its intensity. Or we have grown so much, we don't feel recovery holds anything else for us. There is no room for further growth. And this can happen between Phase 1 and Phase 2 or between Phase 2 and Phase 3. "Is this as good as it gets?" "Did I really come here just to go to all these meetings?" "Surely there's more to this, isn't there?" "I'm sick of always hearing there's something wrong with me!" But boredom is an unrest and a calling forward into the next phase and leads to 3 choices:

1. I think going back to my addiction is a good idea. (WRONG CHOICE)
2. I'm going to stay right where I am. (OK CHOICE)
3. I'm open to the next phase. (BEST CHOICE)

Being 'good' in a phase may prevent discovery or entrance into the next phase.

Fear of letting go of something that's working to step into the unknown, we label all new feelings as bad and we get mixed messages. The next right thing for one person may not be the next right thing for someone else. At the end of the day, The Next Right Thing For Me, has to be the choice. Remember we are only powerless over our addiction not our lives. We are extremely powerful when given back our choice. This is your life, if you don't make your own choices, someone else will, and you may not like their choices for your life.

As you go through the experience of The Great Awakening, there is a certain format you will recognize. I will discuss The 3 Phases of Recovery and will format the information into a principle-based way of thought and action I call The STRENGTH System.

In each phase, I will discuss principles as they relate to each of the letters of the word, STRENGTH. Principles are fundamental truths that are the foundation for a system of belief and reasoning. You will see principles for Phase 1, letters S through H, and the same with Phases 2 and 3.

So, let's get started with our fireside chat that begins with the Phase 1 S's.

Powerless To Powerful Chapter 1. The Phase 1 S's. Solutions, Simple System, and Step #1.

The disease of addiction creates many problems. The list begins with limiting personal and spiritual growth. But it continues with destroying relationships and adversely affecting our physical wellness and mental clarity. When we are in active addiction, proper hydration and nutrition are never a priority, and we lose sight of doing the things in life that make it fun. Addiction becomes our #1 priority and everything else takes its place under that. Remember this, my addiction, your addiction will do anything to keep itself alive!

The disease of addiction is a disease of body, mind and spirit. It manifests itself in all sorts of chaotic and insane circumstances. I could go on and on about the problems it creates. You and I can have a never-ending conversation about how bad it is and all of the problems it causes to you and me personally and professionally. We could go on for hours discussing the problems it causes in our society. Addiction knows no boundaries, it does not discriminate by race, background or social status. The bottom line problem is that the disease of addiction has stolen from me the thing that matters most, my masculine soul. It steals my passion, it steals my purpose. It keeps me stuck in an insane world with limited possibilities and destroys my potential.

You and I can discuss its causes. We can talk about struggles and strains and family history. I can tell you my story, you can tell me yours. But what does that do? You're right, it keeps us focused on the problem. But, here's the deal; if that's all we talk about, we haven't solved anything. So, here's what has to happen.

You and I have to become problem aware and solution focused. The first Phase 1 S is Solutions. Active addiction keeps us focused on a whirlwind of problems. This is a real cause and effect relationship. The insane part of it, is that most people constantly and consistently focus on the effects. How do I know this? I did it. I lived it. I never realized that 75% of my problems would begin to go away (now notice I didn't say immediately) if I would make 1 decision....

Choose To Be Physically Abstinent From Active Addiction! That is the foundation of everything.

This is what I mean when I say, 'cause and effect'. When I look back on my life in active addiction and a majority of the bad things that were happening, these were all of the effects that were manifesting because of 1 primary cause, my active addictions. Being problem aware and solution focused means that instead of focusing on the effects, I choose to focus on the cause. When I focus on the cause and become solution focused, the effects begin to go away.

You ask, "So Mark, what do I have to do to begin becoming solution focused?". The answer is quite simply, "Keep The Primary Thing, The Primary Thing". Albert Einstein once made a statement that can be directly applied to addiction. He said, "The significant problems we face cannot be solved with the same level of thinking it took to create them." Being solution focused means that I accept recovery as a lifestyle and quit fighting addiction.

There was a time in my recovery when I challenged a group of men that I was a part of to do one thing for me; and that thing was, anytime they heard me complaining about a problem, ask me 1 simple question, "Mark, what are you going to do about that?" Focusing on solutions helps me become aware of all kinds of new possibilities. When I am problem focused, I see only the problem. When I am problem aware, and solution focused, I can change the game to one I can win. And you can too!

So, let's talk about the second Phase 1 S. Remember, Phase 1 is The Sustained Physical Abstinence Phase. The second S is for Simple, as in Simple System.

You and I live in a complicated world. A dear friend of mine says all of the time, and I will quote Bill G. here; *"Recovery is a simple program for complicated people"*. And he is right on target. I learned the concept of keeping it simple early on. Back in my letter to you, the reader, at the beginning, I made the statement that I had spent the first 35 years of my life complicating everything and have spent the last 19 years uncomplicating it.

A Simple System can be defined as; *An Easily Understood, Organized Method of Action*. The 2 primary points being; #1 Simple means easily understood, and #2 Action means I have to get moving. I have to do something. I say this all the time and I will say it to you here; Successful recovery is not for people who need it, there are plenty of those. Successful recovery is not for people who want it. There are plenty of those as well. Successful recovery is for people who do it. And this just doesn't apply to recovery, right? It applies to everything else. Results are for those who get themselves into action. Good things don't come to those who wait. Good things come to those who see what they want and get themselves into action to have those things; Good relationships, optimal physical health and mental clarity, more money and the list goes on and on.

You and I can sit here in front of the fire and discuss all the physical changes that happen in our brains, from how the synapses learn to fire to all of the other physiological changes that occur when we quit over-loading our bodies and minds with active addiction. Or we can accept the fact that this works. It has worked for millions before me and will work for millions that come after me. The social proof is there. Understanding the internal workings of a light switch doesn't interest me. I just want the light to come on when I flip the switch. Recovery has been the same way. I have created simple solutions because of an easily understood organized method of action. I acted myself into right thinking. I spent little time worrying about how I felt about it. I saw it working for other men, I did what they did. I saw it not working for other men, I didn't do what they did. I got a sponsor, I worked the 12 steps of 2 different groups (multiple times), I went to meetings, and I realized that this simple system, this easily understood organized method of action works. I wanted the pain to go away and it did. I didn't get caught up in the thickness of thin things, and I came to understand 1 vitally important principle. Let's you and I talk about that now.

It is #3 of The Phase 1 S's. Step #1. The First Step says, "I admitted I am powerless over my addiction and my life has become unmanageable." Let's you and I discuss what that says, and more importantly, what it doesn't say.

Let me begin by saying, as a man, as a former college athlete, as a coach, as a..... you see where I am going with this. My ego does not ever want me to admit I am powerless over anything. The heart of a warrior is part of my masculine soul, and yours too. One of the best ways to get me to do something is to tell me you don't think I can, right? I'll show you! Herein lies the problem. Remember, problem aware and solution focused. Being solution focused is understanding what that first step says, but as importantly how to apply it.

That first step says when I put my addiction first, when it is the primary focus, when it is my priority that I am powerless, and my life is unmanageable. But let me ask you a question. "What happens when you don't put your addiction first?" Now I know you could say that life is still unmanageable. What if you and I made 'The Primary Thing, The Primary Thing', and used our knowledge of what it takes to be successful in Phase 1 In Recovery, the phase of sustained physical abstinence, our primary focus? Am I still powerless? Hardly. Can my life still be unmanageable? Absolutely. But if I am solution focused and have a simple system to use, it is a lot less unmanageable. We can play the game of opposites here. Isn't the opposite of powerless, powerful, and the opposite of unmanageable, manageable?

Now this is just you and I talking. The game here is to decide what we are powerless over and what we are not powerless over. I know for me when I chose life on the positive side of addiction, I also chose to be more proactive and less reactive.

Power comes from being proactive.
Proactive means solution focused action.

I can't use addiction as an excuse anymore. Life in recovery is a prin-ciple-based, solution focused, easily understood organized method of action to help me and you be powerful in our personal and spiritual growth, powerful in our relationships and our careers, powerful in our physical wellness, mental clarity and nutrition, powerful in our recre-ation so we can find that passion to enjoy life.

Addiction renders me powerless, that can be my excuse. Recovery brings me back to the powerful man God created me to be. Guess what? You too! Find your power in being solution focused, create an easily understood, organized method of action and choose to be powerful, in the image and likeness of The One who created you.

Powerless To Powerful Chapter 2. The Phase 1 T's. Take Ownership, Test and Trust.

Over the years I have seen men use all kinds of excuses why recovery wasn't working for them. I have said numerous times, "If you are going to go back to your active addiction, any excuse will do, just pick one." As you and I journey through the information in this book, I just want to tell you, man to man, "Your results, whatever they are, are up to you." When I was in treatment back in 1999, my counselor at the time James L. asked me if I was willing to go to any lengths to stay clean and sober. I only had 1 answer. I was convinced my life depended on that answer. My answer was "Yes, I am willing to do anything!"

I am a firm believer that willingness is the key that opens the door to possibility. It doesn't matter how much information is available, if I am not willing to seek it out, I lose. It doesn't matter how much guidance I receive from others, if I am not willing to act on it, I lose. The first Phase 1 T is Take Ownership. Your question I'm sure is, "Ok, what do I need to take ownership of?" There are 2 items. #1 is you must take ownership of your clean/recovery start date and #2, you must take ownership in your own results.

Successful recovery is a game of personal responsibility.

I can't want this for you more than you want it for yourself. I learned early on, my results were not based on my sponsor, the meetings I attended, my relationships, my career choices, people, places and things. I have to want this and be willing to do what it takes to have this. I have watched men die of cancer and remain clean and sober. Much love to you for your guidance, Mickey F. I have watched men go back to active addiction over a flat tire.

Keeping 'The Primary Thing, The Primary Thing' is based solely on me. And again, calling it like it is, to you, man to man, solely on you. I have been fortunate as an aftercare group leader and as a member of AA and NA, to have helped hundreds of people celebrate milestones in recovery. Every time someone gets a chip, it is an affirmation that this person has taken ownership of their recovery clean date. It is also an affirmation for those who see this, to see that it works. I have told everyone, from men I have sponsored, to men who have gone through my coaching programs and people at events and workshops I have hosted how important it is to get a chip as a celebration for you and to be an example to others. We're going to talk about emotions when you and I discuss The Phase 1 E's but let me tell you right here; Learning to create and attach positive emotions to your results is a must. Things I feel good about I want more of. You and I have spent so much time in the physical, emotional and spiritual pain of addiction, we have to learn to create and celebrate the positive. Even if that positive is just not choosing the negative.

Going from Powerless To Powerful is a choice. It is a proactive choice of personal responsibility. Taking ownership of my clean date and taking ownership of my results and adopting that "Yes, I am willing", mentality is a must. I have had men over the years say to me, "I want what you got", my answer is always, "Be willing to do what I have done". Complaining about results you are not having for actions you are not taking, never works. I am willing, I have taken ownership. Man, to man, you should too!

The second Phase 1 T is Test. Everything I do in recovery is a test. A test of my willingness, a test of my purpose, a test of my priorities, a test of my persistence. Every test is a pass / fail. Pass the test, I get to go on to the next test. This progress is the essence of personal growth, right? Fail the test and I get to start over.

I am grateful I have never chosen to relapse back into active addiction. I have watched men over the years who have. It is sad to watch men relapse once and all of the physical, mental and spiritual pain that are the result of that choice. And what's worse is to have witnessed how it seems to become easier and easier with each relapse.

Willing to go to any lengths means passing the test, no matter how big or small; flat tires, angry wives, bad bosses, death of a loved one, financial distress, just to name a few.

The pain for failing the test is huge. Fail and you start over. You start over a little wiser, but here is the one thing that I have always understood; there's no guarantee after a relapse that I would make it back. The harsh reality, and again, as we sit here chatting about this; let's not paint it any way other than what it is. Active addiction will eventually lead to death. Death of the spirit. Death of the mind. Death of the body.

The rewards for passing the tests are huge, too. Courage is not the absence of fear but the willingness to act in spite of it. Overcoming adversity takes courage. Courage opens up new possibilities. New possibilities awaken the masculine soul to the great potential within. Addiction kills my self-worth, the courage to overcome adversity renews self-worth that leads to a powerful man that makes powerful decisions.

The final 'T' in Phase 1 is Trust. Faith is a powerful word. Faith implies a belief in something. I can have faith in a Higher Power. I can have a faith that recovery works. The examples of it are everywhere. Faith doesn't guarantee me or entitle me to anything. So where am I going with this? You have heard the saying, 'Faith without works is dead', right? That's where I am going. Back to the principles of willingness and action. Faith is great to have, but here is one thing greater than faith.... Trust.

Trust means I am willing to act on what I have faith in.

My faith in a recovery community only works if I am an active member of that community. Trust means I will do what it takes to pass the test. Trust means I will do what it takes to elevate my personal growth to pass the next test, and the one after that. Trust is a principle of action. Faith without works is dead. Faith in action, which I will tell you is the definition of trust, creates results.

But here's the kicker. Just because I trust, meaning I put my faith to work, doesn't always guarantee that I will make the right decision. Making the right decision will not always happen. Making a decision and making it right is what happens when in that 3rd step, I turn my will and my life over to God. God did not put me on earth to always make right decisions. But he did put me on earth to make a decision and if it didn't turn out right, make it right. God says, "Mark, all the good stuff is out here!". I have to trust to go out there. So far, so good, it has worked for me. I'm convinced it will work for you too.

Powerless To Powerful Chapter 3. The Phase 1 R's.
Relationships and Results.

As you and I sit here, God continues to tell me to remind you that Phase 1 is The Sustained Physical Abstinence Phase. This phase is where our lives seem to improve when some things are removed, #1 being the source of so much pain, our active addiction. The first of The Phase 1 R's is one of the most integral parts of life on the positive side of addiction. Learning this simple lesson of addition and subtraction can be the foundation to realizing the promise of peace. Not learning this lesson, especially for men in Phase 1 can have us living free from active addiction and miserable, or at worst, be the driving force back to the pit. I know you're saying, "Alright, alright, enough already. What is it?".

It's relationships.

For the first Phase 1 'R', you and I are going to discuss Relationships. Not individual relationships. This is not marriage counseling It's not therapy. We are not going to discuss our parents, our spouses and partners, our kids or our co-workers. What you and I are going to discuss is a macro view, the birds-eye view of relationships based on 1 simple criteria. And here it is, 3 levels of relationships; Negative, Neutral and Positive. Now I know you are already reeling them off in your mind and labeling the people you know as positive or negative, right? Let's talk about what seems to be the easy one first; the neutral ones.

As I create my simple system it seems the neutral relationships are the easiest ones to cross off the list, right? Well, maybe. Neutral relationships are the ones that I don't give much thought to on the surface. Neutral relationships are the lady who checks us out at the grocery store, the man behind the cash register at the convenience store, someone in traffic, and any other number of what I would call 'casual acquaintances'. Neutral relationships in the long and the short of it, shouldn't have much effect on my day, unless what? I let them. 2 things about neutral relationships. First, how do I let them affect me? A neutral relationship is that person in front of me talking on the phone in the self-checkout line that is taking FOREVER. Do I let this create a negative thought and if it does, do I let it create a negative action? Second, neutral relationships are a test. Remember back to chapter 2, it's all a test. In Chapter 10, The Phase 2 T's, you and I will talk about what I call *The 5 Pillars*. I'll give you a little hint; the first of the 5 is Tolerance.

I know I have mentioned this, that Phase 1 is the addition by subtraction phase. Life improves when we remove things from it, right? Let's look at our negative relationships. A negative relationship is one that belittles, degrades, abuses, invalidates and causes me distress. The negative relationships can be family, they can be someone we thought was a friend, a co-worker, anyone who deliberately or by ignorance or mistake makes it more difficult for me to be successful in the results I choose to have. If you had to look at your relationships and put a negative sign beside the people who really are toxic to you, how many would there be? Now I'm not saying make a list and start crossing people off. Although this one thing really can make a big difference. What I am saying is that if your purpose is to be happy on the positive side of addiction, ask yourself; "Does this person move me closer to that happiness, or farther away from that happiness?" You will see there are definitely people you should spend a whole lot less time with.

On the other side of that coin are the people who inspire and motivate me? These are the people I want to spend more time with. These are the people who are successful at recovery, are successful fathers, husbands, partners and friends. These people want the best for me. These are the people when the chips are down, will support me. These are the people willing to tell me the truth.

My life as a man, your life as a man can be defined by the types of relationships we have.

As kids, our parents told us to be careful who we hung around with, right? Well, let me ask you; "Do you do that as an adult?". In the next chapter you and I are going to discuss 'being an example of 1 of 2 kinds of people'. Do the people you spend most of your time with move you toward positive empowering thoughts and actions? If they do, spend more time with them.

The second Phase 1 R is something you and I have already touched on several times... Results.

So, if you picture a triangle. And this triangle looks like the 'play' button on an audio or video. On the top left point is the word 'Thoughts'. On the bottom left point is the word 'Actions'. On the right point, the word 'Results'. Results are another word for purpose. What is my purpose, what are the results I choose to create? I always tell men I am working with to begin with the end in mind. Have a purpose, have a reason why you are doing something. You may want to ask me this question, I get this all the time. "Which comes first, the positive thought or the positive action?" That's a complicated question and here's why.

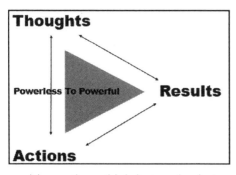

If you were to take that same triangle and draw an arrow from the word 'thought' to the word 'action' and another arrow from 'action' to the word 'result', you can see the progression. I have a positive thought, which leads to a positive action which in turn leads to a positive result. But you could also draw an arrow from 'action' to 'thought' to 'result', right? In essence you could begin with the result. Draw an arrow to 'thought' or an arrow to 'action'. Truth is, there is no right way.

Some people think their way into right action. Some act their way into right thinking. Some stumble into results having no idea what they are doing and create a positive thought pattern and positive actions because of it. But hear what I am going to tell you right now. I know, I told you we were going to have a fireside chat and I wasn't going to preach or talk at you. But, I'm going to do it one time. Thoughts, actions and results are all important, but whatever you do;

Learn To Change The Language You Use To Yourself.

Think about that for a moment. You as a man would never put up with allowing someone to talk to your kids, your wife, your friends the way you talk to you.

Begin here. Instead of being your own biggest critic, be your biggest cheerleader. The golden rule says, 'do unto others', right? As what? 'you would have them do unto you'. The 'do unto you' comes first. Be kind (that's another one of *The 5 Pillars*) to yourself. Spend more time around people who inspire and motivate, and less time with the other ones. The language you use to and about yourself should be consistent with the power of the image and likeness of The One you were created like.

Powerless To Powerful Chapter 4. The Phase 1 E's. Emotions, Example and Easy Does It.

Pain and pleasure are the 2 greatest human motivators. We are supposed to move away from pain and toward pleasure. This is where addiction gets weird. In the beginning, the addiction brought about some sort of pleasure and satisfaction. In the end, it lies to us. It tells us it will make the pain go away and the pain becomes more intense. Suffering is when we sit in the pain. It is the insanity of active addiction. It's a pain we can't seem to let go of and won't move away from.

When you truly understand it, there are really only two emotions, negative ones and positive ones. Put fear, worry, panic, sadness, loneliness and the laundry list of others that make you feel bad in the folder titled, 'Negative'. And put the positive ones like happiness, joy, peace, abundance and any others that make you feel good in the folder titled, 'Positive'. Two emotions; positive, the ones that make us feel good and negative the ones that make us feel bad.

The first of The Phase 1 E's is Emotions. The game is to control your emotions and not be controlled by your emotions. So much of what I see men struggle with is the simple fact that there is some pain on the positive side of addiction. Breaking the bondage of addiction has a price to be paid. The difference is that the pain in recovery makes us uncomfortable. Doing things, I don't like or don't feel like doing is the price I pay for breaking free from the chain of addiction. Let me tell you what I mean.

In the previous chapter we talked about thoughts, actions and results. You asked, "Mark, which comes first?" My answer seemed complicated in its simplicity. So, let me expand on it here. When I look at having a purpose, beginning with the end in mind and creating the results I choose, the entire game comes down to understanding my emotions. Let me say it simply; For me to be successful in my recovery, I have to learn to attach positive emotions to the results I want. But here is what must be understood. You want me to be honest, right? I mean at this point; you and I have a relationship that is based on something we both agree on.... I want the same thing for you I want for myself. I want to be happy and I want you to be happy.

The truth of the matter is if my end result is to be happy, I may have to be willing to do some things that are uncomfortable. I may have to even do some things I don't like. But if I focus on the end result being my happiness, meaning a present moment emotion based on my satisfaction with life, what price am I willing to pay? I know there is pain in recovery. It's not the kind of pain that's going to kill me. The pain in active addiction was going to take me out.

I tell men all the time,

"You have to strengthen your recovery muscles."

Recovery, like physical exercise, strengthens our muscles, but in a different way. Take a man like me who loves to go to the gym and exercise. There is a positive emotion that is attached to both the exercise and the result for having exercised. Then take a man who hates going to the gym, but he does it anyway. Why? Because the result he wants is a healthy body. Guess what, he and I can get the same results, right? Recovery is the same way. You don't have to like going to a meeting or having a sponsor or working the steps, but if the end result you want is a happy, passionate, purposeful life on the positive side of addiction, you'll do it anyway. When I love the result, I am willing to go through the process. When positive emotions are attached to the results I want, man, I'm in. The price paid is worth the reward provided.

The second Phase 1 E, you and I already touched on briefly. It is Example. The guy who was actually my second sponsor, Chris W. (love you my friend and thank you), told me point blank, and I'm going to tell you the same way. In my experience this worked for me so here it is for you to try on. I asked him to be my sponsor at the end of my first year of recovery. Why? For this very reason. He said to me,

"You are going to be an example of 1 of 2 kinds of people; Someone recovery works for, or somebody it doesn't work for. And the choice is up to you!"

He expanded on that when he said (now remember, this was 18 years ago, and I can hear it just like it was yesterday), "There are really only 2 kinds of people, those who teach us how to act and those who teach us how NOT to act, and you should be thankful for both kinds." You talk about keeping it simple. This applied then and this applies now. I know the example I choose to be. You? I know I don't do it perfectly, but I am better today at being an example than at any time in my past. Why is that? Let's you and I talk about E #3.

The 3rd E in Phase 1 is Easy Does It. We hear that all the time, but what does that mean? I have to remember I am not going to fix 20 years' worth of active addiction in 20 days. Won't even scratch the surface in 20 months, but here is what I do know. In creating a simple system, you remember what that means right? A simple system is an easily understood, organized method of action. In creating my simple system, I have to understand that this transformation of my body, my mind and my spirit is a process. I'm not going to be better by the end of next week and neither are you. This is a process of personal growth that truly has no ending. The more I learn, the more I realize there is more to learn. The more I experience, the more I realize there is to experience in the abundance God has created for me, and yes, for you too.

Easy does it means understanding that it is a process and the game is progress in the process. Not perfection. Remember, God didn't put me on earth to always make right decisions. He put me here to make decisions to learn from and if they don't turn out right, make them right.

Progress in the process, being an example of a man recovery works for and learning to attach positive emotions to your results is what The Phase 1 E's are all about.

Powerless To Powerful Chapter 5. The Phase 1 N's. Next Right Thing and New.

My goal here in our sit down is to be effective and efficient at answering any questions you have about life on the positive side of addiction. I would tell you, "I want to shorten your learning curve, provide you information that has you learning lessons in less time than it took me." In saying that, some of these chapters will be longer, some will be shorter. I learn easy in bullet points and try to coach and talk the same way; concise, precise and effective. We live in a complicated world, God speaks to me and I learn not in the complexities, but in what is easily understood and applied.

Back in the last chapter, I told you about a couple things my sponsor Chris W. said to me. Some of the most profound things I have ever learned have been the simplest. The first of the Phase 1 N's is Next Right Thing. I have had the question asked me many times over the years, "Mark, what is the next right thing?" Well here is a simple bullet points answer.

- Chris W. told me that I was a grown man and I knew the difference between right and wrong. And I will tell you, you do too.
- I know in Phase 1 in recovery, the Next Right Thing at the foundation is to "Keep The Primary Thing, The Primary Thing"
- The Next Right Thing has to be the Next Right Thing for my recovery if I am to have a chance.
- The Next Right Thing is to take ownership of my results.
- The Next Right Thing is to live on purpose without violating the rights of another.
- On the flipside; Most men know the Next Right Thing, few will choose the Next Right Thing.

That is all. Simple, concise, effective; These are the Next Right Things.

The second Phase 1 N is the word New. You and I have already discussed attaching positive emotions to the results we want, right? I learned something early on when someone said to me, "Mark, be comfortable being confused.". Today, I know that was something that I needed to hear. Why? This recovery thing was a new experience for me. Here's what I had to learn; I was going to a place I had never been before, so I wasn't going to know how I was going to feel in the process.

Our emotions face backwards. What this means is that everything we feel is based on a previous experience. Our conscious and subconscious minds reach backwards into the files of our mind to try and find an association for a current experience. As humans, it is instinctive in us to have a sort of fight or flight mentality to things that are new. If we don't understand something, we have a tendency to label it as scary or bad, when in fact, the real feeling should be exciting and new.

Recovery is about new experiences. Don't label these as scary, label them as exciting. Remember, you must control your emotions, not be controlled by them. Exciting is a positive emotion, scary is a negative emotion. *The Great Awakening of The Masculine Soul* is a journey for the adventurous, not the timid. Reframe scary to exciting and Do It. Success is not for those who need it or want it, it's for those who Do It!

Powerless To Powerful Chapter 6. The Phase 1 G's. Gift of Desperation, Growth, and Gratitude.

I was and am convinced my addiction was going to end my life. Even today, over 19 years of one day at a times, I still view my journey in recovery as a life and death proposition. I decided to write this book to share my experience and my strength in the hope that any man who is struggling with his recovery can find a message;

If you are willing to do what it takes to change your body, your mind and your spirit to get over an addiction, you can accomplish anything.

In our connection through this information, I sure don't want you to think my journey has been easy. I have had my struggles. I have dealt with the physical, mental and spiritual pains of life in active addiction and I have dealt with the physical, mental and spiritual pain of life in recovery.

The first of The Phase 1 G's is something I heard a man say getting his chip one time. Stafford M. seemed to be a fixture at a lot of meetings I went to early on. He said that he was given the Gift of Desperation. This is our first Phase 1 G. I understood clearly the gift of desperation. Apparently, I had been given it too. Desperation is hopelessness. Your question, "Mark, why are you grateful for hopelessness?"

The gift of desperation has done 2 things for me. At the end of active addiction, this degree of hopelessness made me willing to search for a different way. I can remember like it was yesterday when I said, "God, I don't care what happens, I can't live like this anymore." That total surrender for me was because I was given the gift of desperation. The gig was up, all my options were gone, I was alone with my addiction and I had 2 choices, death or life. I am grateful for the choice I made.

I can look back on it now, my active addiction and see many times where God was giving me hints along the way. "Hey, Mark, it's time to look at this.", seemed to be a tap on the shoulder, a pull on the ear, the gentle urgings I am convinced we all get. I felt abandoned by God but looking back I can see all of the messages I ignored, until.... I had to have my feet knocked from under me. Apparently for me, the gift of desperation was the only way I was going to listen.

I had to be so miserable and so hopeless that my only choice was, "I don't care what it is as long as it's not THIS". Willingness, surrender, the gift of desperation.

There is a term used in recovery, Euphoric Recall. Euphoric recall is when being removed from so much pain, I can forget its intensity. Remember earlier when I said my addiction, your addiction will do anything to keep itself alive? One of its tricks is euphoric recall. It can have a man like me, remembering and romancing the good times in addiction. It tries to convince me it wasn't as bad as it was. It can have me forgetting the broken promises, the sleepless nights, the shaking hands, the panic attacks, the trips to the hospital and the doctor. That is the second thing the Gift of Desperation has done for me; it helps me remember the reality of what my life was, and I am convinced can be again, in active addiction. I am so grateful for the gift of desperation. It is a gift that has me remember what I have to remember to 'Keep The Primary Thing, The Primary Thing'. "I can't and won't do THAT, anymore", opens up all the possibilities on the positive side of addiction.

The second of the Phase 1 G's is Growth. As you and I sit here, relaxed, having an honest and open conversation, there are so many things we have discussed and are going to discuss. All of it has a central message. That message is personal growth. All things stem from personal growth. I was telling you earlier about the concept of 'cause and effect'. What most men do is spend all their time trying to fix all the effects. Personal growth fixes the causes and the effects take care of themselves. Recovery is an inside job. I fix everything out there, by fixing the one thing that matters most in here... my masculine soul. The Great Awakening is a journey of perpetual and continual growth. I can only go to the next place by outgrowing my present place. I made it to recovery because I chose to outgrow my addiction. My relationships are better not because of balance, but because of growth, as are other areas of my life. Not perfect, but better.

You and I are on a journey through the 3 Distinct Phases of Recovery. I make it to Phase 2 when I outgrow Phase 1, and Phase 3 is there as my Discovery and Life's Purpose Phase when I become ready. Remember this; addiction is cunning and baffling. There will be periods of boredom, discontent and complacency in recovery.

Addiction wants you to think recovery holds nothing else for you. It will tell you, "This is as good as it gets." It's a liar. An addiction will do anything to keep itself alive.

When you arrive at boredom, discontent and complacency, use it as a call forward. These things are telling you there is something new for you to do. Remember your masculine soul is built for adventure. This is the call into the next adventure. Let your longing for adventure keep you striving forward not settling for 'good enough is good enough'!

The last of the Phase 1 G's is a biggie. Well, let me tell you, IT'S HUGE! You ask, "What is it?" It's Gratitude. Now I could keep you here for several hours discussing gratitude. Being grateful for what I have, has always led me to more things to be grateful for. It began very simply that I found a solution to what was death of my body, mind and spirit.

Remember, Phase 1 is the addition by subtraction phase. My gratitude will actually take on different meanings for me in each of the 3 Distinct Phases of Recovery. For me, I had to begin being grateful for the things that were being removed. I was grateful that my physical addiction to alcohol and drugs had been removed. I was grateful that all of the little games I had to play were gone, too. You know the ones, right? The lying, the hiding, and all the deceptions my addiction used to keep itself alive. Grateful for the Gift of Desperation, right? So, here is what I know about gratitude. It begins with being grateful for the things that have been removed. It continues with being grateful for the course of events, no matter how painful, that brought me to the positive side of addiction. It keeps going as I am grateful for all the things that are good in God in my life, no matter how small. I perpetuate my gratitude as it grows for the life I am creating.

When I discuss the journey, I know I am grateful for my gift of choice and my gift of choice is to be grateful. I am not perfect at it. Remember, progress in the process. More nights than not, before I go to sleep, I think about things I have to be grateful for. More times than not, as I wake and begin my day, I do the same thing. I have a journal that I created for my many programs that has a box for me to write in that says,

'Today, I Am Grateful For..........'

My level of peace is greater when I take time to be present and grateful for all that was, all that is, and all that is going to be.

Powerless To Powerful Chapter 7. The Phase 1 T2. Team

In an earlier discussion, you and I talked about relationships. The negative, neutral and positive ones we all have. I can't tell you enough, how important it is to spend less time with some people and more time with others. This is a lifelong process. I continue to reach and stretch and grow in every area of my life because I have chosen deliberately to surround myself with people who inspire me. The word 'inspire' means *breath*, and in *spirit*. I have a card on my desk that says, "Surround yourself with people who dream bigger than you do", a constant reminder of a deliberate choice I make. This is what The Phase 1 T2 is all about.

The 'T' is for Team. I got to tell you from the depths of my masculine soul,

> *"It is vitally important for you to build a team of people to help you create the results you want to create".*

"So, Mark, who do I need to include on my team?"

There are 3 elements. #1 A Community, #2 A Guide, #3 A Group.

Let's talk about A Community first. A recovery community helps me go from hopeless to hopeful. Why? Because I am able to see the examples of the people that recovery is working for and I am able to witness the struggles of the ones who are still searching. As men, we long for human connection. Remember back to the story of creation from the introduction. God said, "It is not good for man to be alone." I know in my active addiction, I had never felt more alone. The more I built up the wall to keep you out, the more I built my own trap. I was building walls to keep you over there and I found out that I'm the only one in here.

Technology makes it so easy to connect with people today. I love that it can make our world smaller and provide more information, but I also know that it can be a trap as well. We long for human connection. Person to person human connection. That is why being part of a local community is so important. I spent the first part of my life trying to prove to you I was something I was not. Look at the exterior, it's great, but if you only knew what I was feeling inside. Addiction had stolen my soul, but I was going to keep you over there, so you wouldn't find out what I knew. I was scared to be a husband, I was scared to be a dad, I was terrified I might lose, and guess what? I was.

But here's what happened to me in the recovery community. I got to sit at a meeting and not have to prove I was better than you, but I didn't have to feel less than you either. Again, it's a process. Our process is to realize there have been burning bushes all around us, we just have blinders on and can't see them. The message of hope, the message of recovery, the message of strength is everywhere, but I won't find it sitting at home. Successful recovery is not for people who need it, it's not for people who want it, it's for who? Yep, it's for people who do it. Doing it begins with being part of a community.

The second member of my team is a guide. This can be a sponsor, a mentor, a coach. This guide can be someone that works with you for free and then there are those who require compensation. I am grateful to have and continue to have both. It is vitally important in Phase 1 for me to humble myself and ask another man to be my sponsor. As I begin my journey, I know that when I, the student, am ready, the teacher shows up. I know when I turn my will and my life over to the care of God as I understand Him, He will let me know when it is time to stay put or move on. Sponsorship does not have to be for life. You ask, "Mark, how will I know who is right?". Back to the little lesson from

Chris W. "There are 2 kinds of people, those who teach us how to act, those who teach us how not to act". There are plenty of men who can repeat the sayings and know all the jargon. Success in recovery does not always translate to success in life. That's a harsh reality. I don't care how long you have been clean and sober, if you treat your wife bad and you spend no time with your kids, you're broke and can't keep a job, your health is awful, and you seem mad all the time, I'm going to look to connect with someone else.

#3 is what I call my expectation group. This group is a group of men that I let know me and I get to know them.

It is a group that I will learn to tell the truth to, so I can learn to tell the truth to myself. It is a group of men that I will make a commitment to, so I can learn something I had never done before; keep commitments.

But most importantly, it's a group of men who will help me raise my expectations of myself higher than I have been willing to raise myself. It's a group of men who expect me to remain true to my willingness to go to any lengths, keep 'The Primary Thing, The Primary Thing, and hold me accountable. They can't want it more for me than I want it for myself. Just having a group of men to talk to that understand, but more than that, help me be problem aware and solution focused.

Powerless To Powerful Chapter 8. The Phase 1 H's. Hope, HALT, and Higher Power

In all you and I have talked about thus far, the word 'hope' has been used a lot. I went from hopeless to hopeful when I went from problem focused to solution focused. Hope is an interesting word. For some, it is a reason to move forward. For some, it's a dream that they assume is for others. The first Phase 1 H, is, you guessed it, 'Hope'.

Hope can be a 'want of something to happen'. You know what I said about those who want it, right? The better definition of hope is 'a feeling of expectation that something is going to happen'. Hope shouldn't be a wish, it should be an affirmation. Hope begins with faith and develops into faith in action, which is.... do you remember? Trust. Trust is faith in action. So, when you and I talk, and I say, "My hope for you is", it is not a wish, not a want, but an affirmation and a feeling of expectation. Hopeless To Hopeful, Powerless To Powerful, the first Phase 1 'H', is Hope.

Addiction is a disease of body, mind and spirit. Recovery should also be of body, mind and spirit. I can't tell you how many meetings I have been to and have listened to a man talk about how crazy his mind is and how bad he feels. Being the professional noticer I am (let me tell you, it's both a blessing and a curse), it is amazing that this admittedly insane guy is on his third cup of coffee in the meeting and was chain smoking outside and came in the meeting throwing out a bag of fast food he just had on the way to the meeting. You can see where I'm going with this, right?

I hope (my want of something right, hahahaha) you don't think I am criticizing, because I am not. But, here's the deal. Oh, before I do, let me say the second Phase 1 H is HALT, the letters for hungry, angry, lonely and tired. I'm telling you all that to make a point. We have to learn to take care of ourselves physically. Not having proper nutrition and hydration and not having enough rest will take a crazy addict mind and make it crazier. As a certified health coach, I know the importance of nutrition and rest.

In addiction, a great many of us have done so much damage to our bodies. We have to learn to stack the deck in our favor. The mental and emotional strain of what it takes to create positive accelerated change is challenge enough without us making it more of a challenge with no rest and awful nutrition habits. Again, it's a about progress in the process, but you have to learn to control the controllables. Begin with being good to yourself, get enough rest and improve your nutrition. What affects the body affects the mind, what affects the mind affects the spirit.

The 3rd H in Phase 1 is Higher Power. I know this is an area of struggle for many men. In *The Great Awakening of The Masculine Soul*, it will be hard to accept the fact that you were born in the image and likeness of a creator you don't believe exists. I have never struggled with the idea of a Higher Power. As we sit around and chat about this, you see very clearly, I choose to call my Higher Power, God. I am not looking to write a politically correct book that speaks to every man in recovery. I know that willingness and open mindedness have been two very important principles in my recovery, but I won't spend any time trying to convince a man to change his beliefs or lack thereof.

I have always known there was a Higher Power. To me, it seems pretty simple to understand that I, nor anyone I knew could have created the sunrises, sunsets, mountains, rivers and streams. I couldn't create the birds and the animals, and guess what, neither can you. So, for me, it doesn't take a top-level thinker to admit, there is something greater than me that did.

I know many men have felt like I did. I know a lot of men felt like they have been abandoned by God. Let me reframe this into what I feel really is the issue. Me in active addiction felt unworthy of a relationship with God and it was just easier to assume God checked out on me. What I know now, is that I created a wall between me and God, just like I did between me and every other relationship I had. God didn't check out, He was simply waiting for me to take the wall down.

You heard me mention a friend of mine earlier, Bill G. He has been a great mentor, guide and friend. I heard him one time getting a chip say something that has made my relationship with God much more powerful. It has also increased my effectiveness to share and help other men with their relationship with God. Bill said,

"I am grateful to the God of my understanding, but I am more grateful to the God that is beyond my understanding...."

Think about that for a moment. Think about the power that statement has when I go to work the steps. It gives me permission to comprehend God working in my life, but more, and I feel most importantly, it gives me permission to not have to fully understand God to believe in God. WOW!

Earlier I spoke about growth, now about God. I know that for me, my addiction had separated me from God. Recovery awakened my masculine soul as I began a renewed relationship with God. I know that my relationship with God, just like my relationships with others, is stronger because of my personal and spiritual growth. I know today, that God works through people. God speaks to me through others and I hope I can be a conduit for God in my connection with you. I know that within each of us is a piece of the truest essence of pure love. Part of that is in me, part of it is in you and part of it is in every other human being whether we like them or not. The totality of that love is God. I am incapable of finding God without you. When God said in the story of creation, "It is not good for man to be alone.", that is what He meant. I am quite certain God is the tie that binds us when we are together. God is here, may you find Him now.

Powerless To Powerful. The Beginning of Phase 2. The Rebuilding Phase

So, here we are at the end of Phase 1, which, you guessed it, is the beginning of Phase 2. Remember Phase 1 was the addition by subtraction phase. Our lives improve when we remove several things; the primary one, the use of our active addiction.

Phase 2 is The Rebuilding Phase. It begins the addition by addition phase. This is where we begin to rebuild the life that was crumbled by our addiction. Just so you and I are clear, there really is not a timeframe when you transition from phase to phase. Some people can remain clean and sober for a lifetime and never transition past Phase 1, and there is nothing wrong with that. "Don't use and go to meetings' works for them. Many men carry around the idea that "At least I didn't pick up and use today", is success enough. I get that.

If that is good enough for you, I'd probably at this point, tell you to not waste your time with any more information here. Like I have said several times, "There is a whole lot more to it for a guy like me", and I bet there is for you too. The beginning of my second year in recovery, my world was falling apart. I didn't use and went to meetings, but I had other stuff I had to fix. At that point, I realized what was meant by the saying, "You only have to change 1 thing. And that was ...... EVERYTHING!"

Phase 2 is inclusive of Phase 1, so all the information applies. You and I still have to make sure we keep 'The Primary Thing, The Primary Thing'. Sustained physical abstinence is a must.

Looking back on my journey in the early years of my recovery and being able to chart the path and the progress I was making, I know now there were 8 areas of my life that needed attention. I have created, in my programs, a concept called *The 8 Points Circle of Life*. This concept provides men a chance to take a snapshot of their current circumstances in 8 key areas; Personal Growth, Relationships, Finances, Physical Health, Mental Clarity, Nutrition, Recreation and Spiritual Connection. And as with their recovery, become problem aware and solution focused. Not only does it take a snapshot of current circumstances, it begins the process of creating positive incremental improvement in each of these areas. And again, there is only 1 part of it that matters ... All Of It!

More About The 8 Points Circle of Life at PowerlessToPowerful-TheBook.com

My goal in life, my will, is to be happy, healthy and abundant. I know that's what God's will is for me in my life too. Later, on this journey, you and I are going to discuss 'Happiness'. For now, and I'm sure you will hear me reference this many times, know that;

'Happiness' is a present moment emotion based on satisfaction with life.

Happiness and peace are the result of doing the things that bring them about. They are the result of a well-rounded life that focuses on personal growth and brings about a more powerful spiritual connection. Phase 2 begins the process of rebuilding our relationships, our finances, our physical health and mental clarity, making positive nutrition choices and focusing on our recreation, which is spending time doing the things that make life fun with the people we care about. It's a lot more than just accepting clean and sober as 'good enough'. *Powerless To Powerful, The Great Awakening of The Masculine Soul*, has been created for men who will not settle for anything less than living passionate and powerful in the image and likeness of The Source of All Abundance.

Phase 1 is where we take care of the physical abstinence. Phase 2 is where you and I begin taking care of everything else. Because here my friend, is the harsh reality of it. My addiction was just the effects of the problem. The cause of the problem was the way I was thinking, acting and living. Did I use because I was miserable with the life I was living, or was the life I was living miserable because of my addiction? It's a circle that has no beginning or ending. The simple answer is yes. Which came first? It doesn't really matter. Phase 1, the focus is fixing my addiction. In Phase 2 I have to begin fixing my life. If I don't fix the cause of the addiction, the addiction lays and waits. Remember, it will do anything to keep itself alive.

Powerless To Powerful Chapter 9. The Phase 2 S's. Service and Self-Worth

When I first began my journey on the positive side of addiction, I was a taker. I don't say this as something that is negative. I had to consume information that would provide me a firm foundation on which to build a solid life in recovery. I had to be around givers and I had to be a taker. If you are new, focus on being a taker, too. Connect with people who can help you. Learn to ask for and accept help and guidance.

The first Phase 2 S is Service. As my recovery strengthens and grows, I begin my transition from taker to giver. When I first got started, I had nothing to give. As I gained a little experience and put a little quality with my quantity, I began to understand the spiritual connection that is being of service to another human being. Being able to listen to another and share with them my experience is what makes the magic happen. Nothing gives a guy with 6 days clean more hope than an inspiring conversation with a guy who is 6 months clean and can say, "Man, I know how you feel. I felt like that too. Here's what I did'. The thera-peutic value of 1 addict helping another, in a true 'pay it forward' level of service is what makes recovery work.

Here is one of the challenges of recovery as it relates to service. Not all service is free. I know for me, there was a lot more for me than 'just don't use and go to a meeting'. I have spent a lot of time, money and energy reading books, going to workshops, being involved in coaching programs, having 1 on 1 coaches, going to webinars and live events. All of these have definitely impacted positively the quality of my recovery. I share lots of information in groups, I give away lots of free stuff, but there are people like you who buy my books, get involved in my programs and my events. I'm going to tell you as it relates to recovery;

spend what you can to positively impact your quality of recovery. The investment in yourself will pay huge dividends.

Be willing to tell your story to individuals and groups. It's not difficult. It can be a little scary at first. Be truthful. Don't talk to somebody about working the steps if you haven't worked them. Don't tell another man what he has to do to stay clean and sober if you are not doing it yourself. Being of service is a personal responsibility. Create results and all you have to do is be able to say, this is what it was like, this is what happened, and this is what is like now. Share your success with others. One of the greatest levels of service you can be is to get a chip at a meeting. That is affirmation to a person with less time than you that they can do it to.

So, what would be the one question you want to ask me about service? Shoot. "Mark, what is the best level of service I can provide?" Great question. While there is a multitude of ways to be of service in recovery. You can show up early and greet people and set up chairs. You can chair meetings and be on the service boards. You can sponsor men and guide them through the steps. I can go on and on.

Here is what I feel is the greatest service that you can be to someone who is sick and suffering from the disease of addiction.... Be An Example of Someone Who No Longer Suffers!

The second Phase 2 S is Self-Worth. Let me differentiate something here. I am not talking about self-image. Having a positive self-image is the result of personal growth and positive choice. Self-image is how I see myself, my self-worth is my value. I must build a positive powerful self-image, I must accept my self-worth. *The Great Awakening Of The Masculine Soul* is the awareness that I was born in the image and likeness of my Creator. And so were you.

Here is something that I have put in my programs for men to understand. Your addiction is not who you were, and it is not who you are, it is what you did. Let that sink in. I know I had to. Although there were things I did that I am not proud of, they were what I did. I take personal responsibility for them, but my value is not tied to that. My value, my life, my masculine soul and my self-worth comes from the Almighty. I'm a child of God who made bad decisions because of my addictive thinking. Negative labels create negative values. No self-worth leads to negative self-image. Worthiness is God-given. You were born in His Image and Likeness. You were born worthy, you must learn to accept your worthiness.

Accept your God-given worthiness today. I did, and I do every single day. Some days it's easier to know and feel the value placed on me and in me by my Creator, but it is given whether I accept it or not. Same with you. It is amazing what happened to me when I finally made peace with the fact that I didn't have to work for this worthiness. Think about the value of a diamond. Whether it is in a ring for people to admire or whether it is lost in a mud pit, it is still a precious stone. Your self-worth is the same. Your value is real whether on display or temporarily lost. When I talk about accepting the abundance God has to offer us, the first thing to accept is self-worth. He gave it, I got it, you got it too.

Powerless To Powerful Chapter 10. The Phase 2 T. Transformation

Alright, we're fixing to get into some important stuff here. Let me warn you, this is one of the longest chapters and is full of information.

When I make the statement, that 'there is a lot more for me to do than just don't use and go to a meeting', my journey through Phase 2 is where I began to realize this. When I did my personal inventory in Step 4 and shared that with another man in Step 5, two very important things happened. First, I was able to see that my defects of character were choices I made, so I just had to make better choices. Second, and thank you Mike M, for helping me see this, my personal inventory wasn't just the bad stuff. It contained some good stuff too.

When I was in treatment in 1999, my counselor, James L., had me do a little exercise. He had me go to the chapel and write out the 10 attributes of the man I aspired to be. He also told me that when I got stuck, sit still and listen to God. So, I did that. Pen and paper, I sat and listened to God and came up with my list. Next, he had me share that list with my group the following day. I was so proud of my list. I had put down all of the things that I wanted as a man, a husband, a father, a son, a brother, a friend and a businessman. I actually had written down 11, being the overachiever, I wanted everyone to think I was. I got done sharing these things with the group and James asked me one profound question; "Mark, what are you doing to be that guy?". That question just floored me, because I knew the answer. I thought, "My whole life is a lie. The way I act is not how I aspire to be."

The Phase 2 T is Transformation.

The definition of Transformation is; A Thorough and Dramatic Change

In our discussion thus far, you have heard me use the word, process. Out of all of the extremely important words that are part of the make-up of a successful life on the positive side of addiction, process, is among the most important to understand. Everything is a process. A process is 'a series of actions or steps to achieve a particular end'. The 'particular end' means I have a purpose. My purpose in Phase 1 is to take a series of actions or steps to build a solid foundation of sustained physical abstinence. This begins a dramatic change in my body, my mind and my spirit.

Phase 2 begins the 'thorough' part. Being thorough means 'complete with regard to every detail'. I just wanted the pain of active addiction to go away. Complete, with regard to every detail, required me to take an honest look at everything else. I am constantly reminded of the phrase; 'sometimes quickly, sometimes slowly, they will always materialize if I work for them'. This is the process of my transformation that requires me to be thorough. If I fix the physical abstinence thing, but I don't fix the mental and spiritual thing, I have completely missed what recovery promises me. When I did that little exercise in treatment I just told you about, and worked steps 4-9, it became apparent to me, I had a problem with the way I was living.

So, how did I fix it? First, let me tell you; I am still in the process. Not everything is perfect, but it's a whole lot better. I am definitely not the man I used to be and a whole lot closer to the man I aspire to be. Second, and this is what began my Phase 2 Transformation;

I started applying 'One Day At A Time To Everything Else'.

Here's what I figured out. I have mentioned several times, this recovery thing had to work for me. I viewed this as a life and death scenario. If

I do that 3rd Step correctly where I turn my will and my life over to the care of God as I understand Him, and He shows me the path to deal with this addiction thing, and it works. Why wouldn't I apply that same level of thought and action to everything else? Notice here, I didn't say "God Fixed It". I said, "He Shows Me The Path". God is not going to do this for me. My transformation is up to me. He puts the right people, the right circumstances, the right information in front of me when I become problem aware, solution focused and willing to act. So here are the 8 areas I focused on. Again, I call these *The 8 Points Circle of Life.*

#1 Personal Growth.

The personal development / self-help industry has grown by leaps and bounds over the last 19 years I have spent on the positive side of addiction. The process of building a successful life in recovery is the ultimate personal growth platform. What I have learned and have taught now for over 17 years is the principle of learned optimism. We live in a world that is full of learned helplessness. Unfortunately, many who adopt this, 'the problem is always me, I have this disease, if I only got what I deserved, I'm just an addict, I don't have any expectations, I'm just grateful I didn't use today' level of thought and action, will never raise their awareness to the new possibilities of abundance that is available to them.

Success rates for men in recovery are just like success rates in everything else, extremely low. Why? Here's the deal; Let's just call it what it is; few are willing to pay the price. When a man I am working with says, "I want what you got", my answer is always, "Be willing to do what I do". Listen, this isn't complicated. The same information that has been available to me over the last 19 years was available to the guy who relapsed until he died. The same information is available to you. My job is to help you compress time and get it quicker than I did. Have I arrived? Hardly. The more I learn, the more I realize there is to learn.

Personal growth is a game of personal responsibility. Your masculine soul is worth fighting for. You must accept the fact that God created you powerful, this is your self-worth. Then you must go about building a positive self-image that is the reflection of your value.

Your value to the world, to your community, to your family and friends will never reach its full potential until you value yourself.

Accepting your powerful self-worth is *The Great Awakening of The Masculine Soul.* Transforming your self-image is your personal responsibility in recovery. Success is the process of incremental positive change. Incremental positive change is the result of learning to attach positive emotions to the results I want and transforming my thoughts and actions to make those results a reality.

#2 Relationships

In Phase 1 Chapter 3 you and I discussed relationships. We kept it simple right? 3 levels of relationship, negative, neutral and positive. Spend less time around some people and more time around others. Pretty simple, pretty effective. In the next chapter, we are also going into relationships in greater detail. Here, I want to tell you 1 thing I had to learn ... and man it hurt when I did.

Up until I made it to recovery, everything in my life was a big deal. It was either a good big deal and my ego wanted you to see how great I was. Or, it was a bad big deal, and guess what, that was always somebody else's fault. If it worked, it was me. If it failed, it was someone else. And this applied to everything. My struggle in my marriage was 'her fault', a bad business deal was 'his fault'. I blamed my addiction on lots of people too. Blame is a game of learned helplessness, a totally powerless proposition for positive results. The exact opposite of blame is personal responsibility. God didn't put me on this earth to always make right decisions, but He did put me here to make a decision and if it doesn't turn out right, make it right. I am still in the process, over 19 years later of taking personal responsibility to make things right.

The 1 thing I had to learn about relationships is that if I want to be in the right one, it wasn't up to me to find the right one, but to BE THE RIGHT ONE. And that applies to every relationship. Now listen, this is not the place where I say, "all my fault", or 'all my success'. I have done, and am still doing, the work on me, to take personal responsibility for my stuff. I carry the consequences of failed relationships, but I have a powerful self-worth and an improving self-image, that I don't own anyone else's stuff. We come to recovery and identify ourselves with some problems. We adopt a learned helplessness that we in these rooms have a problem and everyone out there is 'normal'. Let me let you in on a secret; "They're screwed up to".

Everybody has something they are struggling with. 2 imperfect halves don't add up to a whole. 2 imperfect people brought together won't have a perfect relationship. There is no, perfect. But in order to be in the right relationship, I have to focus on being 'the right guy'. We are broken people traveling on broken roads. I must put God at the center of my relationships and take personal responsibility for transforming myself into 'the right guy'.

#3 Finances

Wow, right? I am not qualified to give anyone financial advice. Somehow, I learned how to make a lot of money, but that didn't translate on how to have or keep a lot of money. This book is not about teaching you about your personal finances. I know, a great many of us come to recovery in a bad financial place. I know I did. And for me 2 years in, it got worse. Divorce and bankruptcy happened. But here is what I know, and it's back to that one day at a time thing.

If I want different results, I have to make different choices. I know for me, the career I had chosen had to change. I know for me, I had to transform the way I thought about my finances. They were just like my alcohol and drug use; I'll deal with it tomorrow. I had to adopt the concept that better decisions bring about better results. There is no way I could fix my financial issues as fast as I wanted to. But, I also realized, I would never fix them if I didn't begin at some point. As with anything else, success begins with taking the first step. Results happen when I make progress in the process. My first sponsor told me that I could fill in the hole the same way I dug the hole, a shovel full at a time. He was right.

#4 Physical Wellness

The disease of addiction is one of body, mind and spirit. You've heard me say that a number of times. The solutions of recovery must also be of body mind and spirit. I know for me; my active addiction was really taking a toll on my body. I was in constant pain, the consequences of a body overloaded with pills and booze. As a certified health coach, I have always helped men realize the path to good health is also a process. We can't go back and fix all of the bad choices we made regarding our health. We can't go back and fix the choices of misplaced priorities and neglect when it comes to our physical health. We can't make a better past, but we can begin today, creating a better future.

Here is what I decided, and I hope you decide this too. If I wasn't going to let active addiction kill me, I wasn't going to let bad health choices in other areas kill me either. I quit smokeless tobacco 6 months in and have remained physically abstinent from that too. Let me scare you a little. I have watched several people I loved and cared about deeply die in recovery because of the abuse they put their bodies through in active addiction. #1, it is heartbreaking for someone finally to give up their addiction for the disease to kill them in recovery. You must care enough about the temple that houses your spirit to take care of it. Remember Phase 1 is the addition by subtraction phase. Your physical health improves because you quit doing a few things. Phase 2 is the addition by addition phase. Physical Wellness is the result of being proactive with your health.

#5 Mental Clarity

A short bit ago, you listened to me tell you about the exercise my counselor had me do while I was in treatment. In his instructions to me, he said, "Sit still and listen to God." This had such a powerful impact on me then and still does today. This was such a powerful experience for me. It was my first go at meditation and I never realized it until sometime later. It was the first time in who knows how long that I emptied my mind of all of the chaotic thoughts I was having.

Mental clarity is the result of several things. Meditation helps. It helped me then and today, as I have made it one of my positive addictions. I have learned to control my thoughts and not be held hostage by them. I keep meditation, like I do everything else, simple. For me, meditation is not absence of thought, it's controlling thought. It is where I can sit still and learn the difference between truth and illusion. I didn't write this book to be a lesson in meditation. I can meditate and listen to God anywhere I choose. I spend time every morning when I wake and every night before I go to bed. I meditate when I am riding on my tractor, when I exercise and any number of places that I calm my mind and listen.

Mental clarity is also the result of doing the right things. Learning to tell and live in the truth brings about mental clarity and relieve mental anguish. The disease of addiction, being a disease of the mind, as well as body and spirit, has us living in the world of illusion. I know for me, I had to tell 5 lies to cover up 1. The perpetual game of hide and seek in addiction is mentally exhausting. Learning to live a principle-based life in recovery gets rid of the games and has us living in peace not panic. Having to remember all the lies we tell will create a chaotic thought process that is just awful. Peace for me was the result of going to meetings and working the steps in Phase 1. Continued peace for me means

I am making the right decisions in the other areas of my life as well. Want to drive yourself crazy in recovery? Know the right thing to do and don't do it. Keep lying, keep playing the games, keep the addictive thought process and you may stay clean.... and miserable.

#6 Nutrition

I could write an entire book about nutrition for men in recovery. In my programs, I constantly help men focus on all 3 aspects, body, mind and spirit. Which one is most important? The answer is, "Yes!" Remember back to my story about the countless number of men I have witnessed coming into a meeting talking about how crazy they are? After 3 huge cups of caffeine, a pack of nicotine, and a belly full of food additives, no wonder, right?

When I am doing coaching sessions with men and they say, "Mark, man, I just feel crazy today!". I have them immediately play back what they have consumed for their nutrition, first. If a guy drinks coffee and energy drinks and doesn't have enough clean pure water for hydration, that's where we start. Are you taking medication for your allergies? Have you had plenty of protein, some vegetables and fruit?

As kids, we heard; "You are what you eat." What are you today? Does it matter? "Not just yes, but, HELL YES IT MATTERS!" Understand this. When we put down our addiction, our body goes through all kinds of physical and emotional changes. So, 5 cups of coffee in recovery will have a different effect on you than 5 cups of coffee did in active addiction. Now listen, I'm a guy, I'm a meat and potatoes guy. But the fact is, my nutrition in all phases of my recovery matters. It took me some time to create the pivot points necessary to learn to live right and eat right. And again, it's a process. Phase 2 is the Transformation Phase. Everything is in transition, everything is a process. Know that, there is only 1 part of it that matters, 'ALL OF IT'!

#7 Recreation

All work and no play makes Mark a dull boy. When Mark is a dull boy, his mind tells him active addiction is a good idea. I was addicted to booze and pills. I was addicted to many other things too, none more corrosive to the life I wanted to live than work. I was addicted to busyness, I was addicted to complexity. I had to work long hours that kept me away from my family. I traded all of that for an addiction to effectiveness.

We as men, are consumed with an ego attached to hard work. I get it, I spent years in the construction business addicted to the adrenaline rushes and the game of 'then next big deal'. I love to work on my farm and get dirt under my fingernails.

What I learned, as I transformed my life in Phase 2 of my recovery was that releasing this 'working hard, working long' ego and replacing it with 'working effective' was a better choice. Now don't get me wrong, I still have to do hard work, but my ego and self-image is not attached to it. I still have bills to pay and I still have to generate an income. The transformation for me began early on when I realized that my career was a source of my addiction. I drank and drugged myself to sleep because I had gotten to a point where my career consumed me. I let it ruin my marriage and it was going to ruin my ability to be the #1 influence in the lives of my kids. I had bills to pay, but God put me on this earth to be a really good father.

When I transformed my thinking, I realigned my priorities. When I realigned my priorities, I realized that I could create a harmony between, spending time doing the things in life that make it fun with the ones I love, and my career. I actually could have them both. I need time to recharge my batteries. You should too. I had a tough time admitting that my addiction to work covered up my fear of being a husband and a father. That was a biggie for me. I hid behind work and I can also hide behind my recovery. In Phase 2 I learned that sometimes I need to spend time with my kids instead of going to a meeting. I need to take the love of my life to dinner. All of this is about recreation, but it positively effects the relationships I have with the ones who matter most. Again, it all matters.

#8 Spiritual Connection

"Having had a spiritual awakening as a result of........" Anyone? You got it! ".....working these steps. There is no coincidence in the way I lay out my programs. It begins with personal growth and ends with spiritual connection. But guess what, that's not the end. Spiritual connection leads me to the desire for more personal growth. This is a circular journey. The end leads to new beginnings.

Spiritual connection for me begins with my acceptance of the powerful self-worth God gave me when I was created. Spiritual connection continues for me as a build a positive powerful self-image and through a process become the best version of me I can be. Whether you know it or not, God's will for you is the same as your will for you. God's will for me is perfect happiness. My ever-expanding relationship with the God of my understanding, and the God beyond my understanding had me realize that all along this journey I have been in a fight with God. He is trying to provide for me a life of abundance and perfect happiness and I have been doing my part to keep that from happening. Not intentionally, but it is my doing nonetheless.

Every man that was ever born has a purpose. Your #1 purpose in life is the same as mine.

My #1 Purpose In Life Is To Find My #1 Purpose.

When I turn my will and my life over to a Power greater than me, I have to find a harmony with that Power. My struggles and failures in my previous careers have led me to what I do today. I thought my tombstone was supposed to read, "The Greatest Real Estate Developer and General Contractor Ever". God had a different plan. I like His plan better. I love creating resources to help men where I was. I was problem aware, solution focused and willing to act. Today, I know, God's purpose for me is my purpose for me too. It is both powerful and humbling as well.

Powerless To Powerful Chapter 11. The Phase 2 R. Relationships & The 5 Pillars

In the last chapter, you and I discussed transformation. Rebuilding the life, we crumbled in our addiction requires a thorough and dramatic positive change in the 8 areas we discussed. As it relates to relationships in Phase 2, our focus becomes, what I call The 5 Pillars. These pillars provide essential support for our life on the positive side of addiction. Each is essential. Without one of these pillars your structure lacks the integrity to stand powerful in the image and likeness of our Creator.

Find Out More About The 5 Pillars at PowerlessToPowerfulThe-Book.com

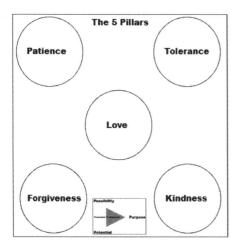

As you and I go through each of the 5, there is 1 important thing to realize; Having these is the result of practicing these in all of our affairs. What I mean is this; Praying for these doesn't mean God will grant me these, but what He will grant me, is opportunities to practice these.

Pillar #1 Patience

The first of The 5 Pillars is patience. Patience is the ability to accept something without frustration or anger. The ability to accept a situation doesn't mean I have to like the situation. Our addictive minds want immediate gratification. Learning to be patient with others helps us learn to be patient with ourselves. I must avoid frustration and anger like I would the plague. When I ask God to give me patience, I better be ready. What I get is opportunities that require my patience. I pray for patience, God gives me the lady in front of me in line at the grocery with 2 kids, a cellphone and 25 items in the 15 or less line. I pray for patience, God gives me a funeral procession when I am late going somewhere. Patience is a muscle that gets stronger with use. Patience happens when I live life in the moment and not in a chaotic frenzy. Patience is peace.

Pillar #2 Tolerance

I heard a guy in recovery say one time, "I am an ego maniac with an inferiority complex." That's really funny but think about that as it relates to life in active addiction. One of the greatest gifts going to 12 step meetings taught me is the principle of tolerance. The recovery community is diverse, right? We come in all shapes and sizes, both genders, all colors and backgrounds. Addiction is not selective. One of the greatest messages in the recovery community is 'principles before personalities'. Remember my definition of ego? Things I want you to see about me that I really don't like about myself. I had spent the better part of my life trying to prove to you, I was someone I wasn't. Today, at a 12-step meeting I can be tolerant of you, because I have done the work to be tolerant of myself. I can sit next to you today and not have to prove that I am better than you. But more importantly, I can sit there and not feel less than you either.

Pillar #3 Forgiveness

Alright, here we go. Forgiveness. Does that word make your skin crawl? For many of us it did. If you are anything like me, you had said, "I'm sorry" so many times they quit counting. If you are anything like me, "I'm sorry. No, I really am this time. I mean it. I promise", is a phrase I said so many times I quit counting. Our actions in active addiction creates so many circumstances both short term and long term for which we must seek forgiveness. Rebuilding relationships in recovery is tricky. I learned very quickly, just because I was finally free from active addiction, the world didn't line up to applaud and forgive me.

There are several things I have to understand about forgiveness. The first is the word empathy. Empathy is the ability to understand how someone else feels. I put the people around me in a bad place because of my addiction. When I finally made it to recovery, I guess I expected them to just turn the page. Unfortunately, it doesn't work that way. Recovery has taught me to slow down and try and see the world through someone else's experience. I remember like it was yesterday, when Horace W. heard me complaining about an issue me and my ex-wife were having, and he said, "It's about time you go to an Al-Anon meeting so you can see what you put her through." You know what? He was right. I went to several family group meetings and I listened empathetically to what those people had been through. Grateful for the guidance of men like Horace, I sure needed it.

The second thing I have to understand about forgiveness is that it can't be on my terms and on my time. When I did that 8th step and 'became willing to make amends to them all', I realized my willingness doesn't always bring about someone's willingness to wipe the slate clean. I have listened to guys over the years say, "I'm clean and sober. I did what she wanted me to. How the hell can she not forgive me?" Sound familiar? Yeah, me too. I know from experience. My willingness is the key. My willingness to say, "I know I have said I'm sorry hundreds of times when I didn't mean it. This time I hope you can find it in your heart to forgive me". Forgiveness is a process.

Remember this; the best amends I can make is changed behavior!

I could go on for hours about forgiveness. It is so vitally important to rebuilding the lives we crumbled because of our addiction. Forgiveness can be a stumbling block or a stepping stone. But here is what I feel is the most important thing to understand about forgiveness. There are not varying degrees of forgiveness. You either live in it or you don't. When I do my step work, holding on to resentments myself and then trying to figure out why someone doesn't forgive me creates a major disharmony in my internal system. If I can't forgive 100%, how can I expect to be forgiven. Living in forgiveness is freedom. But, here's the kicker about forgiveness.... I have to have done the work on me, that I can forgive the one who I need to forgive the most. Who is that? ME.

Forgiving myself means no more games, no more illusions. Forgiving myself means I can release the past and work on better todays. I forgive myself of all the promises I made that I didn't fulfill, all the dreams and time I squandered, all the mistakes and all the missed opportunities, all the unrealized potential of my past as a man, as a husband, a father and a child of God. When I say the Serenity Prayer and I am grateful for 'The Wisdom To Know The Difference', that wisdom means I have the courage to change the one thing I can, ME! I forgive myself today and you should forgive yourself today too!

Pillar #4 Kindness

When my dad's journey on this earth ended in January of 2018, I can't tell you what a difficult time that was for me. I loved my dad. I never one time considered booze or pills as a means to deal with the pain. He was the dad that would take a red-eye flight to make it home so as not to miss one of my sports events. He was the dad that was involved in everything I did and everything my kids did. He was one of the greatest influencers in my life because of the principle you and I are going to discuss right now. No, it wasn't the fact that he and my mother had the kind of marriage we all strive for because they would both tell you, God is at the center. No, it wasn't the fact that up until his death, he and mom took the time to come see me get every recovery birthday chip that I ever got at the aftercare program where I went to treatment. Yep, 18 times he was there. I can go on and on, but here is the one thing I got as a lesson in life from my dad.

Be Kind, No Matter What

At his visitation and funeral, I couldn't begin to tell you how many times I heard, "I loved your dad, he was the kindest man I ever knew". One guy sent me an email that said, "I always admired your dad because he was the only person who was kind to me when I couldn't do anything for him." What a legacy, huh? There are only two kinds of people. Those who show us how to act and those who show us how not to act. Thanks Pop, for showing me that I can be kind, no matter what!

Pillar #5 Love

1 Corinthians 13:13.... and the greatest of these is Love. Here is what I know about my concept of God. I don't ask that you adopt this as your own, but hope you find this to strengthen your connection. God works through people. I think too often we are waiting for a sign from God, that shows up in people. He shows up in burning bushes all around us and we just keep going through life with our blinders on asking, "God, Where Are You?"

When we raise our awareness and take our blinders off, we realize there are burning bushes everywhere, just like the people who God is working through. I know for me, God shows up in conversations I have, books I read and social media posts. I know God shows up when I am ready because I know God is always ready. Every single person in this world has within them the essence of the purest love of God. It doesn't matter who they are, from the pulpit to under the bridge, there is a piece of this love in each of us. The totality of that love is God. That's why we long for human connection. Connection with positive powerful people reveals what we want from ourselves. We want to live in God's glory and it is found through connecting God's love in our families, our communities and our world. I say It all the time when it comes to recovery; "God is here, keep coming back until you find Him!"

Powerless To Powerful Chapter 12. The Phase 2 E. Enthusiasm

Enthusiasm means to have an intense passion for something. Throughout our time together, you will hear me use the words enthusiasm and passion interchangeably. These are two of my favorite words. Why? Because, my life in recovery has ignited an enthusiasm and a passion in my masculine soul that addiction was stealing from me. It doesn't matter whether you are addicted to booze and pills, gambling, pornography or one of the addictions our society celebrates, like work, your addiction is stealing it from you as well. And here's one that will really surprise you.... recovery can as well. How do I know? It is part of my story.

Our world today is filled with many illusions about true masculinity. Masculinity is misused by men and misunderstood by women. False masculinity uses force, not God-given power. False masculinity is passed down to our sons by ignorant men who don't understand it either. Now listen, I am not using the word ignorant as a means for me to judge anyone. Let me be the first to put my hand in the air and say, "I was missing it, too!" We celebrate men for their touchdowns on Sunday and their bank accounts on Monday and view the illusion of life as an MMA fighter as true masculinity. Why is that? Because we haven't been guided to focusing on what is real; God-given, God-inspired masculinity.

So, here's a question; Does the guy who competes to catch the winning touchdown pass on Sunday afternoon compete equally as hard to be a good husband and father? Here's several for you; Do you have as much passion for your marriage as you do for your fantasy football draft? Does it show? Do you care as much about your son being a Godly man as you do about your golf game on Saturday? Do you ever take your daughter on a date instead of spending 2 more hours at the office?

Here is what my life on the positive side of addiction has taught me. I mentioned it in the introduction; I am in a battle for my masculine soul! This surrender thing is great when I surrender my addictions, but there is a battle going on inside me and inside you that we better understand... and more than that, win!

You have heard me many times say that we as men were born for adventure, right? I mean deep down in our masculine soul is a wildness that loves adventure. Adventure is different for each of us. You don't have to sit in a tree stand at sunrise, go on a climbing expedition, run with the bulls or stand waist deep in freezing waters looking out over a decoy spread to find adventure. Adventure is the essence of competition. You as a man, me as a man were created adventurous. We were created competitive. God made us that way.

The problem is, and this is where the backlash of ignorance begins, most of us are competing for the wrong things. And it's on full display to the world. Are we looking for a misguided false masculine conquest? Or are we focused on *The Great Awakening of The Masculine Soul* that has us enthusiastic and passionate winners in our personal growth and our spiritual connection?

I'll never forget the day my wife at the time said to me, "You were never home when you were drinking and you're never home now, so what's the difference?" You know what? She was right. I was fighting for the wrong things in my addiction and I needed to have this wakeup call, so I could create a pivot point in my recovery. It was a painful lesson that I had to learn. My transformation in Phase 2 had me create pivot points when I become problem aware, solution focused and willing to act. Guys, our women need to know they matter. They need to know we are ready to battle for them. And so do our kids.

I don't hang my head and say," I'm just an addict". Today, I am enthusiastic and passionate and 100% positively addicted to a relationship with a woman I love who also loves me. I am addicted to being a great dad. I have an enthusiasm and a passion for my spiritual connection and my career choice. I am enthusiastic and passionately addicted to my life.

I played 3 sports all the way from age 7 through high school. I played 2 sports in junior college and was fortunate to have had the opportunity to play at a 4-year school as well. My whole life was built around Mark, the athlete. I remember like it was yesterday, when my college career ended, and I hung up my gear for the last time and it was truly over.... I was lost. The man I had created was no longer there. The things I competed for my whole life were gone. Now, I had always been the kind of guy that wanted the ball when the game was on the line. Let me be the one to shoot the free-throw, throw the ball to me in the endzone, let me be at the plate with bases loaded and 2 outs in the bottom of the ninth. I thrived on enthusiasm and passion. I knew I had what it takes. But when it was time to step away and step into life as a husband, father and businessman, what happened? I was terrified that I didn't have what it takes. What my family needed was an enthusiastic passionate husband and father, I focused on work. I was willing to fight, it was just for the wrong things. In came my addiction.

I am a firm believer that my addiction was the pivot point of my life. I have 3 grown children. 2 confident Christian young men and 1 confident Christian young woman. Both of my boys were great athletes. Through my journey in recovery, I was able to help them learn a lesson I never learned as a young man... sports is something we do, it is not who we are. Society today, through its warped concept of misunderstood masculinity, is adopting an attitude that winning doesn't matter. Let me tell you winning does matter as long as we are striving to win at the right things. Young men need to be raised to learn to compete for what matters and understand why.

If you are new to recovery,

WIN the game of sustained physical abstinence first, then WIN the game of everything else!

If you have been around awhile, discover a new energy level. Be addicted to the positive stuff. Enthusiasm and passion are a choice that become habit. If you are feeling bored with recovery, that is not a call backward. It's a call forward. There is a new enthusiasm and passion waiting for you. It's a new level of service or you could write a book. Do something to keep recovery fresh and life exciting. I always say, "If you are willing to do what it takes to change your body, mind and spirit to get over an addiction, you can do anything. Just get started!"

Powerless To Powerful Chapter 13. The Phase 2 N. Nature or Nurture

This has been a highly debated topic that has been around a lot longer than I have been in recovery. A couple of chapters ago, I warned you on the frontend about what was one of the longest chapters. Here I am going to tell you, this is one of the shortest conversations you and I will have. Why? Because I like to be effective. On this topic, you and I having a long drawn out conversation does not make the information more understandable. Albert Einstein once said, "If you cannot explain it simply enough, you probably don't understand it!". With the topic of Nature or Nurture this holds true.

So, the question you have is; "Is the disease of addiction hereditary?" The answer is, "Yes....... and No". "Wait, what?" That's not an answer, it's an opinion. You can talk to as many experts as you want, and you will get some 'yes' and some 'no'. I am going to give you a more practical answer.... that's actually a question, "Does it really matter?" And then the statement I always make regarding this, "There's no solution for me knowing the answer to that question."

My grandfather was, my dad wasn't, I am, my brother isn't. Is it in our family? Yes. Is it because of heredity? I think it's because of the choices I made. Here is what I know. The disease of addiction is a family disease, not because the whole family has a chance to have it. It's a family disease because it affects the entire family. But, here is what I also know. The solutions of recovery affect the entire family as well.

There is no sense in me wasting my time figuring out why. It's like I tell my kids all the time, "It doesn't matter what happens and why, what is important is what you do about it". I know for me, I am better in every area of my life than I probably would have been had it not been for the adversity of my addiction. It created in me a resilience and a strength, I may not have otherwise had. I would probably not be writing books and creating resources, coaching programs and events had I not found my path and my purpose through my addiction. So, here's my suggestion, take what you like and leave the rest, but you asked. "Don't get caught up in the thickness of thin things." Wasting time trying to figure out if I can blame this deal on my grandfather is a waste of time. I take personal responsibility for having it, and I take personal responsibility for what I do with it, and you should too.

Powerless To Powerful Chapter 14. The Phase 2 G. Goals.

A goal is a desired result. What does it mean to have a goal? To have a goal, means I have something I have set my sights on. It means I have a why, a reason, a purpose to do or have something. As men, you and I understand, we live in a world where goals are important. Going from Powerless To Powerful begins with having a goal, having a purpose. When I have a purpose, I will raise my awareness to new possibilities and awaken my unlimited God-given potential to make those possibilities a reality. Remember this, aiming for only general improvement will bring marginal results. Let me explain how this relates.

Phase 1 is the sustained physical abstinence phase, right? When I began my journey, I had a goal to stay free from active addiction one day at a time. My goal was 1 week, then it was a month, then 3 months and so on. I had a goal; to stay physically abstinent. I had a why; because I was tired of living the way I was living, and I wanted to live more than I wanted to die. I had a reason; because I loved my kids. A dear friend of mine told me one time and thank you John B. for your friendship and help on more levels than you will ever know, that there will come a point when I will stop staying clean and sober for what was chasing me and learn to stay clean and sober for what is in front of me." Think for a moment how simple, yet, how profound that statement is.

In Phase 2, my recovery goals must transform if everything else is going to. In Phase 2, remaining physically abstinent from my active addiction is a must, but it cannot remain as my only goal if I want to rebuild my life. Now listen, I am not belittling anyone if their only goal for the rest of their life, is to just stay clean for today. If that works for them, that's great. There's a lot more to it for me and I know, you too.

At some point, that goal is only general improvement and will bring about marginal results.

I am grateful that I learned early on my journey that God was promising me a lot more than just physical abstinence and a life defined by just 'less misery'.

So, what does that mean, and how does it relate to what we have discussed so far? Let's you and I talk about goals, growth and values.

First, let's talk about growth. Growth is the process of creating results. The results I desired began happening when I began to transform my thoughts and actions... 'a spiritual awakening as the result of these steps'. Growth means I have a reason to set a goal, set the goal, do what it takes to make that goal a reality, then have a reason to set a bigger goal. Now listen. I am not looking to have you think this is a complicated process. Too many men are never goal getters because they create a process so complicated they actually sabotage their own results. For me, keeping it simple is a must. But if I am going to rebuild my life in Phase 2, and then discover and create a life on my terms in Phase 3, my goals have to grow as I do. If my goals don't grow, neither do I. In Phase 1, I went from a day at a time to the days at a time adding up. In Phase 2, I have to focus on everything else.

Other than not having goals and having goals that are not progressive in your process, the biggest stumbling block is having goals that don't honor your values. In my *P2PThirty Program* and also in my *More Powerful Me Membership,* I have created an entire training module focused on goals and values. It is a solution focused training that identifies that the most powerful goals a man can set are the ones that are in harmony with his values. The bottom line is this; goals that honor your values work, goals that don't honor your values won't.

For More Info On Goals and Values Go To; PowerlessToPowerful-TheBook.com

Earlier I told you the story of the 10 attributes exercise my counselor had me do in treatment. You may have thought, "I wonder what they were.". Well, here you go. Before I give them to you, I want you to know, I just opened my desk drawer and grabbed them. That's right! That exercise had such a huge impact on me, I kept these from 1999, to refer back to. So, these are the attributes of the man I aspire to be. Remember, God helped me with this list when I sat still and listened. Here they are; spiritual, serene, courageous, grateful, sincere, wise, patient, caring, humble, responsible and forgiving. That is the man I aspire to be.

Those 11 attributes are values. My Phase 1 goal of sustained physical abstinence was achieved because the goal was aligned with my values. And guess what? The goals I have in Phase 2 as they relate to my personal growth, my relationships, my finances, my physical wellness and mental clarity, my nutrition, my recreation and my spiritual connection are also aligned with these values. Make your 'why' is so huge that you will be courageous enough to focus on the 'how'. Steal the ones off my list, add to it, or create your own list. But I know and will tell you from experience, goals that are in harmony with my values are where I receive the promises of recovery that are a lot more than just 'less misery'. The values God has me understand, makes the easy times awesome and the difficult times worth going through. This is not always easy. It's simple. What is most important.... It Is Always Worth It!

Powerless To Powerful Chapter 15. The Phase 2 T2's. Time and Trust

The first Phase 2 T in this chapter is Time. Time is one of the craziest aspects to understand in recovery. In Phase 1, I had to learn to stay clear of active addiction, one day at a time. In Phase 2, I had to learn to apply this to everything else. As it relates to Phase 2, many men I have worked with struggle with time and the expectations surrounding time. Let me be the first to tell you, the chances of you rebuilding your life from 10 years of active addiction in 10 months, isn't going to happen.

I know for me, I had to focus on the quality of my time not the quantity. If I focus on the quality, the quantity takes care of itself. I think that is one of the most important aspects of going from Powerless To Power-ful. It's not about how much time I accumulate, but the man I become in the process. I have been around men who have a couple decades of quantity, but I was just amazed at their lack of quality. I didn't want anything they had to offer. But that's just for me. They were obviously doing something right in their recovery, but something was amiss in how it translated to being a powerful Godly man. On the flipside, I have been around men who inspire and motivate me who have been in re-covery for 90 days. There is a man who was recently part of one of my programs, Carson B. He has tried unsuccessfully a couple of times, but this time he has really got it happening in his life because of the man he is in his recovery. I want everything he's got!

Looking back over my time in recovery and being able to be part of so many other men's journey as well, I can see that there are times that seem to signify opportunities for real personal growth. In Phase 2 for me, it was at years 2, 6 and 9. They are different for everyone, but I do know this. The times for extreme growth, begin with adversity. It's really sad to watch a guy get bored and feel recovery has nothing more to offer him that he convinces himself he can go back to his addiction successfully. For me, boredom and discontent has always been a call forward. I know when I feel I have outgrown where I am, it is time for me to up my game. Life always has more to offer because of successful recovery. If I had gotten derailed when adversity hit me, you and I wouldn't be having this chat right now. The call, the urging is always forward never back. God invites us into *The Great Awakening of Our Masculine Soul*. It is up to us to answer that call.

The second Phase 2 T in this chapter is Trust. As it relates to the first T of this chapter, Trust takes time. The harsh reality I had, was the simple fact that now, just because I was in recovery, didn't mean everyone trusts me. Again, I couldn't have the expectation that now, freedom from active addiction entitled me to anything, most of all someone else's trust. I can't tell you how many times I have heard guys say, "I can't believe she doesn't trust me, I'm doing everything I am supposed to be doing. Geez!". And how many times I've said, "You've only been doing it for 30 days. How long were you in active addiction?"

Trust is something that is earned, and again, something that I am not entitled to. I work the steps, I ask for forgiveness, I make progress in becoming the man I aspire to be. But, truth be told, there is some trust that is broken that can never be fixed. Choices I made in active addiction, made me untrustworthy. I have to set in motion the process of becoming trustworthy.

One of my 11 attributes was 'responsible'. Being responsible means being trustworthy. I have to be that regardless of whether or not trust I have broken in relationships can ever be mended or returned. Just like when I make my amends. I have to ask for forgiveness whether the person grants me that forgiveness or not. There was a guy in my aftercare group, his name was David. I don't remember his last name or initial, but I remember something he said. "My goal is to be able to walk down the street and not have to duck my head and hide from someone because of something I did." To me, that is the result of becoming trustworthy. Cleaning up the wreckage of the addictive consequences allows me to live in the abundance God offers me on the positive side of my addiction.

So here is the lesson I had to learn. Be trustworthy whether they trust me or not. At the end of the day, I can walk down the street, head held high with a positive powerful self-image knowing I was born in the image and likeness of my Creator and I am focused on being the best most trustworthy version of me I can become. Not perfect, but better today than I was yesterday, but not as good as I will be tomorrow.

Powerless To Powerful Chapter 16. The Phase 2 H's. Humility and Habit

Humility is one of the most misunderstood words in a man's recovery process. It is also one of the most misunderstood words in a man's life. There are 2 sides of humility and we are going to talk about them both. There is false humility and then there is true humility. One is of God and honors God, one is not. Any guesses?

When I was in active addiction, I had no true humility. Ego and true humility mix like oil and water. An addiction does anything to keep itself alive and being humble is not only challenging, but highly unlikely. A view of false humility is the idea of weakness and low self-worth and value. Men view being humble as tucking their tail between their legs and accepting, reluctantly anything the world is willing to give. When I finally make it to recovery, false humility has me buy into the idea that 'I am just an addict and if I only got what I deserved......' You've witnessed this, right?

Humility doesn't signify weakness. True humility signifies strength. That is why it is the first of The Phase 2 H's. Remember problem aware, solution focused and willing to act. I have to humbly admit that there is a problem, but true humility means I only accept that, because I am willing to live in the solution and do something about it. I told you a few chapters back, recovery is a powerful personal growth platform. Growth begins when I become problem aware, but to think that to continue on being labeled by my problem is a good thing, is crazy.

True humility is of God. I can accept that there are some chinks in my armor, but I better also be willing to accept that God gave me that armor to be a spiritual warrior.

True humility means I am willing to accept my greatness. My self-worth was given me to be a powerful image and likeness of my Creator. When God says, "Mark, why are you hiding over there behind that tree?" False humility, is me saying, "Well, you know God, I am an alcoholic and a drug addict'" What's God's answer? "Ok, you can stay over there, but all the good stuff is out here."

True humility means I quit hiding, quit posing, quit accepting my problems as who I am. True humility means I take personal responsibility for what I did. True humility means I take personal responsibility for my past. But stand back! Here is what happens. When I accept that, I have to learn to accept this. True humility means I accept God's purpose for my recovery and find God's purpose for my life. True humility means I am solution focused and open to new possibilities. True humility means I know without any doubt, I was created by Him as a powerful message from Him with an unlimited potential to honor Him being the best version of me.

The second Phase 2 H is habit. A habit is defined as a settled tendency. Habits take time to develop and time to change. Habits can be both negative and positive, right? I can have a negative habit that turns into a drug addiction and I can have a positive habit that is exercise.

Now you and I can discuss what it takes to create or break a habit. We can go into discussing the circuitry of the brain and the time it takes to 'rewire our thoughts' so we can take better actions. There is a real physiology to this.

But, here's what helped me more than anything else when it came to break the cycle of my negative habit of addiction. Instead of thinking about quitting something, I made a choice to replace it with something else. Addiction is a disease of the body, the mind and the spirit because of the chaos of misplaced priorities. I know for me, I always had the priority of being a good husband, father and business man. My problem was, my addiction was at the top of the list. My addiction, through a series of choices created in me an opportunity for having no choice. My priorities became my addiction, then everything else. Addiction stole my power of choice. Recovery gives me back that power, so I can re-align my priorities. I say all the time, "My addiction is still a priority, I just have so many things in front of it, I never get to it".

When I look at *The 8 Points Circle of Life*, as long as I make my personal growth, my relationships, my finances, my physical wellness and mental clarity, my nutrition, recreation, and spiritual connection my priority, I never make it to my negative addiction. Truth be told, I call the priorities in my life my positive addictions. My positive addictions replaced my negative addictions. I didn't have to quit anything. I'm addicted to a relationship with a woman I love, I don't have time for my negative addictions. I am addicted to being a really good dad, I don't have time for my negative addictions. I am addicted to helping men find God in recovery, I don't have time for my negative addictions. I am addicted to exercise, riding my tractor, my 4-wheeler, sitting in a tree stand, you see where I'm going with this, right? Break your negative addictions by replacing them with the abundance God is offering. It was, and is available to you, just like it was, and is available to me.

Powerless To Powerful. The Beginning of Phase 3. Discovery and Life's Purpose Phase

Here is where it gets interesting. When I said in the letter to the reader, by the end of you getting this information my goal is for you to say, "Yeah, that's the way I want to think too". This is where we were going; to Phase 3. Most men in recovery totally get the concept of Phase 1. I have a problem, I admit the problem, I have to do something about this or I'm going to die. Part of that group gets the concept of Phase 2. My addiction was only a symptom of my problem and I really have to make better decisions about the other areas of my life. The fact that we have to remain physically abstinent is a must. The idea that there is more to be done to get our life back on track stretches us a little but is understandable.

The idea of discovery and life's purpose is the phase you won't hear about at meetings and your sponsor probably doesn't understand it either. Phase 3 is where you discover why you found the positive side of addiction and may even discover that the cause of your addiction was the simple misuse of a power God gave you. In recovery, I have been around some of the most creative and passionate men. When they finally shake free from their negative addictions, this passion in paying forward the message is why recovery communities work.

Now, again, you have heard me say this a number of times; I am not here to judge anyone. Their journey is theirs, mine is mine. My goal again is to give you a path to find God's Purpose, Possibility and Potential. Here is what I discovered once I rebuilt the life that I crumbled because of my addiction.... it was the life I was trying to escape from. My career, my relationships and on and on. I had men telling me to be happy where I was. I heard them tell me to go to another meeting, sponsor some more men. Bottom line Phase 3 for me began when I knew God's purpose for me wasn't in line with what I was doing. God had a bigger purpose for me. You are experiencing this book because I listened, sometimes painfully, sometimes confused by, but never by mistake, to God's call.

My life today is far from perfect. Every day I work to put together my puzzle called 'Life', there is so much I am grateful for. To say I am grateful for my addiction may sound crazy, but I am. To say I am grateful for the things that went away may sound crazy, but I am. God had a purpose for me that was bigger than the life I was rebuilding. He had a purpose for me that took a level of trust, courage and resilience, I never would have had without the lessons learned through addiction and recovery. The things I lost, I learned from. The things I gained, I am grateful for. The broken road I'm on brings with it a passion in my masculine soul like nothing I could have ever imagined. Enjoy your journey through Phase 3. Take what you want and leave the rest. I hope to this point, if you never read or hear another word, it has been worth the price of admission.

Don't quit here. Your best life, the opportunity, To Live A Life You Love is calling you!

Powerless To Powerful Chapter 17. The Phase 3 S. Strength

Let's begin this conversation with the definition and meaning of a couple of words.

'Strength' is the quality of being strong, having power and passion.

'Principle' is a fundamental truth that serves as a foundation for a system of belief that can be universally applied.

Strength is a fundamental truth that men should use as a system of belief and live with power and passion. We live in a society that spends so much time pointing out our faults. Especially for us men. Again, back to the ignorance of true God-given God-inspired masculinity. Look around, you see masculinity criticized everywhere. Just spend a little time watching the news or on social media. Pointing out the faults of men outnumbers pointing out successes at an alarming rate. While most people love a good success story, others would rather point at the defects of others. Why is that? I hate to be the bearer of bad news but think about this. If I spend all my time pointing the finger at someone else, maybe, just maybe, it will take the focus off me, meaning you and others may not see my shortcomings.

Hmmmmm. What if it didn't have to be that way? What if I were to tell you that instead of pointing at the faults of others, I can make the world a better place by wanting for others what I want for myself? What, you ask, do I want for myself? To Live A Life, I Love.

Psychology as a science has always been focused on figuring out what is wrong with us. Without going into a lot of detail, if we only spend time discussing our shortcomings, is there any coincidence why life satisfaction is so low? It seems as though the focus is to figure out what's wrong and repair it to basically bring us back to a base level of just barely miserable. It's like taking our life from -8 to -2. It's better, but does it really help you to Live A Life You Love? The biggest issue seems to be that men have just resolved themselves that this is as good as it gets, let me just make it safely to death and maybe if I make the mark, there is a reward on the other side. Therein lies the problem, our society is beating the masculine soul out of men by stealing their dreams. And it's our fault if we let it happen. But, there is a solution.

There is *The Science For Success* that is based on the parameters of figuring out what is right with me and you. You see each of us was born into this world with an unlimited amount of potential. Now does that mean that I can ever win the New York City Marathon or dunk a basketball like Lebron James or hit a tennis ball like Roger Federer? The answer is no. This unlimited potential plays itself out in a different way in my life. My purpose is different and the strengths I have been given to nurture and use are completely different. And the same goes for you and every other man. We are unique and so are our strengths and talents. So, in a world where we all like to compare ourselves to others, the real challenge unfolds. It's not up to me to try and be like somebody else. It's up to me to be the best version of myself.

The science I am speaking about is Positive Psychology. This is *The Science For Success* because it focuses on our individual strengths. It also focuses on how they are applied to have us create positive powerful versions of ourselves, so we can be impactful in creating positive and accelerated change in ourselves and our communities. It's the road map to take our lives from -2 to +8. I discovered this at the end of my first year in recovery and it changed everything for me. It helped me go from the, "I'm just an alcoholic and addict mentality" to "If I am willing to do what it takes to change my body, my mind and my spirit to get to the positive side of addiction, I can do anything!"

Within all the great philosophical and spiritual traditions, Positive Psychology has identified 6 virtues and 24 accompanying strengths within the virtues.

The virtues are:
1. Knowledge and Wisdom
2. Courage
3. Love and Humanity
4. Justice
5. Temperance
6. Spirituality and Transcendence

Notice the first virtue is knowledge, for my purpose here, as in, gaining and applying. The last one transcendence meaning, life having a higher purpose.

The signature strengths (which back to a previous conversation are 'values') are curiosity, love of learning, open-mindedness (critical thinking), ingenuity (originality), social intelligence, perspective, valor (bravery), perseverance, honesty, kindness (generosity), love (and to be loved), loyalty (teamwork), fairness, leadership, self-control, prudence, humility, appreciation of beauty and excellence, gratitude, future mindedness (hope and optimism), spirituality (sense of purpose), forgiveness (mercy), playfulness (humor), and zest (passion and enthusiasm).

If you are anything like me, you will start an immediate attachment to which of those strengths best defines you. Let me tell you a secret. When I did that, I was so off base. Why? Because I picked the strengths based on how I wanted you to see me, not the strengths that I really have.

More On Signature Strengths at; PowerlessToPowerfulTheBook. com

Most men find that they live their life from a place of 'good enough is good enough'. Why is that? Most men are unaware of the possibilities and unlimited potential that God put in the foundation of their masculine soul. There's nothing wrong with living in 'the good enough', but what if The Life You Love is right on the other side of that. You see, you will get in life barely above what you choose to settle for. What if there really was a place where discovering life's purpose is attained by awakening and living from within your core strengths. These core strengths are *The Great Awakening of The Masculine Soul*. What if God created you for greatness and all you accepted was mediocrity?

Now listen, when I say God created you for greatness, that doesn't have to mean being a successful public figure. But it also means, if that's what you are called to do, do it. When I got to recovery, I never imagined what God's purpose for my recovery and my life was going to be. I know God's will for each of us is perfect happiness. My perfect happiness means I am willing to turn my will and my life over to the care of God as I understand Him. What that means is that I am open and willing. If something is on my heart, I don't question it. The comedian George Carlin once said,

"Those who dance seem crazy to those who can't hear the music".

Think about that. God created you unique. Your value to your family, your community and the world is not between 'you and them'. It's between you and Him! Phase 3 is defined by discovery and purpose. God led you to recovery for a reason. It may not be time to do so now, but don't you think it's a good idea to figure that out? Me too. Just do it! Scared? Do it anyway. Unsure? Do it any way! God has HUGE plans for you. A man's #1 purpose is to find his #1 purpose. Phase 3 is where that magic happens.

Powerless To Powerful Chapter 18. The Phase 3 T. Transcendence

Alright, I'm going to take you on a trip back to high school or college here really quick. At some point, you studied a little bit of psychology, right? In the last chapter I introduced you to something I discovered in the year 2000, the little-known science of positive psychology. I have been passionately studying it and teaching others about it for the last 17+ years. In a Malcolm Gladwell book, he stated that studies have shown that in order to be an expert in anything, it takes roughly 10,000 hours of study. So, I guess, when it comes to positive psychology and recovery, I qualify.

I have been fascinated in how the same information works for some and doesn't for others. I know that while the information can be consistent, the 'human factor' is the greatest variable. The love of my life, Ashley, is also in recovery. You remember me saying how grateful I am for the new things I found, right? She's at the top of my list. She says all the time and it applies here. "Every day is somebody's someday.", when discussing the greatest variable. She has also taught me one of the greatest lessons I have ever learned. It is; Meet People Where They Are.

Maslow's Hierarchy Of Needs

So, back to high school or college, I'm sure at some point you studied Abraham Maslow and the triangle that is the hierarchy of needs, right? The foundation of the triangle being the basic needs to survive; water, food, sleep, etc. The next level is our safety needs of family, health, employment and security. The next level; love, belonging, friendship and sexual intimacy. Next is esteem, confidence and achievement. The top is self-actualization, also known as transcendence. Remembering back to the 6 virtues from last chapter, #6 was transcendence.

So, let's look at our life in active addiction. Just on the base level of the basic survival needs. We chose addiction over food, water and sleep. Is there any reason for me to continue going up the hierarchy? The answer is no. The truth is, in active addiction, we put our addiction in front of every one of our physical, emotional and spiritual needs. In recovery, we have to reverse that process. We begin at the bottom in Phase 1, right? You and I discussed the concept of nutrition and sleep. In Phase 2 we began to focus on the other stuff; our relationships, finances and physical health. We also discussed building a positive powerful self-image because we accepted addiction as 'what we did' not 'who we are' and that our self-worth was an acceptance as we were created in the image and likeness of The Most Powerful.

And now, we have made it to the Phase 3 T. Transcendence. This is the discovery and life's purpose phase. When I tell you that this information, these burning bushes are all around you, this is what I mean. Increasing our awareness to new possibilities means I understand that my awareness is in direct proportion to my willingness. I realize the limitless...... I mean think about that word as it relates to God and what He can do in your life. Limitless potential, without limit, unlimited.

Transcendence is the result of the process. There is a purpose for your recovery. There is a purpose for your life because of your recovery. I don't know what that means for you, but I know what it means for me. I am in a relationship with a woman who knows what it means for her. And our mission is to help men find out what it is for them. I can promise you this, and this is why recovery is such a powerful personal growth tool. Your purpose will always be tied to being of service to others. Look to serve, God will bring you to your purpose. But, the work you have to do on yourself is the journey. This whole deal is about the man I become in the process. Have I arrived? Hardly. I'm just getting started. So, when you hear me say, "I am addicted to life", now you know why.

Powerless To Powerful Chapter 19. The Phase 3 R. Relationships & The Mastermind

Really, relationships again? Yes, absolutely. Relationships are so important for the strength of our recovery and for the purpose we are looking for in our lives. In Phase 1 Chapter 3, you and I discussed the negative, neutral and positive relationships. It's really not hard to recap that, right? Spend more time with some and less with others. In Phase 1 Chapter 7, we talked about the importance of surrounding yourself with a guide, a group and a community that supports your recovery. In Phase 2 Chapter 11, our focus was on The 5 Pillars; Patience, Tolerance, Forgiveness, Kindness and Love. And now, here we are in Phase 3, The Discovery and Life's Purpose Phase. Here you and I are going to discuss The Phase 3 R, Relationships and The Power of The Mastermind.

In his 2 great books, *Think and Grow Rich*, and *Law of Success*, Napoleon Hill gives us the definition of the master mind.

"A mastermind may be created through the bringing together or blending, in a spirit of perfect harmony, of two or more minds. Out of this harmonious blending the chemistry of the mind creates a third mind which may be appropriated and used by one or all of the individual minds. This mastermind will remain available as long as the friendly, harmonious alliance between the individual minds exists.

He goes on to say,

"Two minds will not blend nor, can they be coordinated unless the element of harmony is present, wherein lies the success or failure of practically all business and social partnerships.

The mastermind principle is the driving force behind recovery meetings. "The bringing together or blending is a spirit of perfect harmony". God's message to us in Matthew 18:20 says, "For where two or three gather together in My Name, I am there with them". What is the spirit of perfect harmony? It is to overcome the problems associated with addiction. And guess what? It works, and it has for many decades.

When I said in the intro to Phase 3, that you won't hear about the idea of discovery and life's purpose phase at a meeting, it isn't because there aren't men there who have found their life's purpose because of their recovery. It means that the meeting has a different focus. And when I said, "There's a lot more to it for a guy like me...", that's what I meant. I still go to meetings and I have found my life's purpose because of my recovery. But that is not what I share about at meetings. In Phase 1 I have to be around men whose focus is physical abstinence. I can find that at a meeting. In Phase 2, I have to be around men who help me rebuild the life I crumbled because of my addiction. I can find that at a meeting, but the group just got smaller. Why? Some men are successful with recovery but struggle with how it transitions into life.

Finding God's purpose for your life that is in perfect harmony with what your purpose for your life is, is the result of being around men who understand that both are somehow connected to being of service. Finding this can be a process of what can be viewed as failed attempts. God has allowed me to become just about everything I ever wanted to be. Some of it worked, some of it didn't. In the end, He had a different purpose for me that I found not on the path of recovery, but because of my path in recovery. Again, have I got it all figured out and feel like I have arrived? Absolutely not. My life is a work in progress just like yours.

Have you ever heard the phrase, "I can see as far as I do, because I stand on the shoulders of giants"? That is one of my favorite sayings. I am grateful for all the giants who have helped me see that God's purpose for me was bigger than I was capable of seeing. I know God put these men in my life at just the right time and in just the right sequence. Like the guy who coached football where my kids went to high school. On Friday mornings, the dads would get together to paint the lines on the football field. I was fortunate to have had the opportunity to be part of that group for years. When my oldest son was a senior, it was my job to show up early and coordinate that process. How cool it was to see dads come together because of their choice to be the #1 influence in the lives of their sons. Doing this provided me an added bonus. Friday morning before every home game I got to spend time with Coach Mac. Every man needs a Coach Mac in their lives. He and I would talk very little about football, but spend more time talking about what it takes to raise confident Christian young men into Powerful Godly Men. That, my friend is the God beyond my understanding. The power that awakens my masculine soul will then connect me with the right men who can help shape and guide me into the man God is calling me to become. Let me warn you, the further down this path you travel, the less and less men there are who 'get it'. This journey is not for the timid. It's easier to live in the land of 'good enough is good enough'.

The Power of God working in me and through me happens through a process I call, The Divine Sequence. The Divine Sequence is the sequence of time, resources and most of all men who show up in my life as the result of seemingly random situations. My mind struggles with the why. The why now? This sequence is of God and it is His sequence that guides me. These situations are the power of the Mastermind of God, molding me into the man He needs me to be to serve others. When I, the student am ready, the teacher shows up. The teachers are the giants God has put on the path all along my journey that inspire, motivate and expect great things from me.

If your path has led you to feeling like there is something calling you, there probably is. If your path has other men saying, "Just be happy with where you are", that's more about them than it is about you. Surround yourself with men who think and dream bigger than you do. Surround yourself with men who say, "If you feel it is right, go for it." Mike R. used to say to me all the time, "It only has to make sense to you." My mastermind group has to be made up of Powerful Godly men. Men who understand the masculine soul and will not run or hide from the ignorance of others. I have to surround myself with men who instead of saying, "Why me?", say "Why not me?" God has a calling for me and He has a calling for you. The Power of The Mastermind is the power that will guide you to that calling in the discovery and life's purpose phase of recovery.

Powerless To Powerful Chapter 20. The Phase 3 E. Elevation

God has equipped each of us with a purpose. A purpose for our recovery and a purpose for our life. Whether you know it now or not, whether you feel it now or not, you are part of His Divine Sequence. I mean, look around you. There is so much wrong that needs to be set right in this world. Look at the God-less men running around with all of their egos, their false and mis-guided masculinity. How do I know this? I have been one and can still be one of them. I can edge God out and have to create a pivot-point to get back on track. Look at all of the women out there, criticizing men and masculinity. Why? Because so few have a reference point of what a Powerful Godly man is.

There are passions written on your heart. The wounds of your life, the crosses you have had to bare and overcome. The challenges, the adversities all tell a story of struggle and more importantly, and most importantly, triumph. Men love a good success story. Every movie we watch, every sporting event, everything we do seems to be a struggle of good vs evil. Remember the story of the old Indian man that told his grandson that within every man there is a battle that rages. It is a struggle between two wolves. Think about this as it relates to our struggles with addiction. The first wolf is evil. It is full of hatred, anger, lies, arrogance, jealousy, inferiority, false pride and ego. The second is good. It is full of love, empathy, kindness, forgiveness, tolerance, truth and faith. The young man asks him "Which wolf wins?" The answer, "The one you feed!"

Instead of focusing on 'so much wrong', look instead at all of the opportunity. There is a passion that is burning inside of you to be a man of impact. To be a guy that makes a real difference. God created you that way. How do I know? Because, He created me that way, too. I am certain God puts within every man the desire to courageously battle, to live from a place of passion and realize his own God-given, God-inspired potential. I say all the time, "I choose to be a *More Powerful Me*". Some days I win this battle, some days I learn a lesson to begin the next day a little wiser.

Let's begin this chapter with another definition.

Elevation is a warm positive emotion we get when we observe or interact with someone who is deliberately engaged in acts of kindness and well-being, thus making us want to be better ourselves.

In a recent chapter you and I discussed the little-known science of Positive Psychology. 'Elevation' is a Positive Psychology term I just fell in love with the first time I read it. Matter of fact, Ashley and I call our company, 'The Elevation Project', for that very reason. I saw the 'warm positive emotion' as 'passion'. I saw the 'deliberately engaged in acts of kindness and well-being' as 'having a purpose of service' and 'making us want to be better' as the best 'example'. In short, it is a Powerful Godly Man deliberately being a Powerful Godly Man.

In the beginning of a Dr. Norman Vincent Peale book I experienced, he wrote, that he dedicated this book to his 2 brothers, who he called 'effective helpers of mankind'. Think about that phrase, 'effective helper of mankind'. Could there be a better description of being of service? Having a purpose? Being a Powerful Godly Man? We are all called to be effective helpers of mankind. It's why I tell men all the time; "Don't use your recovery as an 'us against them' and just being a spiritual giant at a meeting. Use your recovery as a way to become better and then pay it forward by being of service."

Remember back in Phase 1, I had to learn to be a taker. In Phase 2, I began learning to give back, be of service to others in recovery. In Phase 3, I am supposed to be a man who is deliberately engaged in acts of kindness and well-being, making those who observe me want to be better themselves. Where does this begin? How about something as simple as picking up a piece of paper instead of stepping over it or grabbing the empty shopping cart on your way into the grocery store. Don't do it so others will notice. Do it because it's the right thing and others will observe and follow suit. When you understand this, you will be amazed at how many opportunities there are to create that warm positive emotion, elevation.

There is 1 other thing to discuss as it relates to this subject. It's great to help others feel good, right? I mean being a man of impact by being an example of all that is good and right in this world, draws us all closer to that perfect love in each of us known as God. Phase 2 Chapter 16, you and I discussed habit and the phrase 'positive addiction'. Elevation for me is a positive addiction not just because of the effects it has on others, but because of the effect it has on ...... You Got It, ME. When I do the right things it's easier to do more of the right things. When I choose powerful thoughts and actions that I know are in harmony with the mind of God, it creates in me an addiction for more of those powerful, positive thoughts and actions.

It's easy to do when someone else goes first. What about you? Are you ready to be a leader of men? Now I'm not talking about creating a movement (but if you need someone to give you permission, I'm in go ahead). I'm talking about being a man who lives in the image and like-ness of our Creator being a man living a powerful, purposeful, passion-ate, principle-based life defined by The 5 Pillars of Patience, Tolerance, Forgiveness, Kindness and Love. It begins simply by being that man at home. Then being that man in your neighborhood. Then being that man in your groups and communities, at school, at church, at the grocery, and on and on. I'm sure when Gandhi said, "Be the change you want to see in the world", he didn't mean wait for another man to go first. He meant be, as in you, as in me, as in now.

My purpose revealed itself after years of striving to do the right thing in spite of the challenges and adversity. I say this again, "I haven't arrived". God sharpens us, as you would sharpen an axe, a swipe at a time. Swipe after swipe, He is preparing us to be willing and then ready to clear a path through all of the world's struggles and be the man in our homes, our communities and the world that makes others want to be better. As bad as it can look, do you see disaster? Or, do you see opportunity? I know what God wants us to see. He sharpens us to be a courageously, passionate, purposeful effective helper of mankind. When I am, when you are, other men will join us. The Phase 3 E is Elevation.

Powerless To Powerful Chapter 21. The Phase 3 N. Now

Some of the most profound things are the simplest to understand. Remember back to our discussion of a simple system, right? It is an easily understood organized method of action. Successful recovery and finding success in life on the positive side of addiction is all about action. Successful people do what unsuccessful people are not willing to do. This goes for recovery. This goes for personal growth. This goes for relationships. This goes for finances, and every other point on *The 8 Points Circle of Life.*

The Serenity Prayer says,

> *God, grant me the serenity to accept the things I cannot change, The courage to change the things I can, And the wisdom to know the difference*

Let's you and I discuss that prayer for a moment.

If you have been around recovery for any length of time, you have heard and repeated that prayer countless numbers of times. Have you ever dissected it and understood what it really means? It is so profound in its simplicity. Profound in Phase 1, Profound in Phase 2. The Phase 3 N is Now, and is right on target, as to what it means to understand the Serenity Prayer.

Let me ask a question and you can only answer with one word. What is one thing you cannot change? Keep it simple, this is important. The answer? Yes, you are right! You cannot change the past. It doesn't matter how bad you want to. It doesn't matter how smart you think you are or are not. It doesn't matter how bad you need to, right? I've been there. I cannot, and you cannot change the past. What I did, I did. The people

I disappointed and hurt in the past, can't change it. The financial struggles in the past, I can't change it. The lost time with my kids in the past, can't change it. You see where I am going, right. The past is the past, I have to make peace with that. Peace is serenity.

Now I'm going to ask you the same question. Again, 1-word answer. You can't use the same word. What is one thing you cannot change? The answer? This one is a little more challenging. Ok, I'll tell you. The future. You can't change the future either. Before you get all bent out of shape, let me explain. The past can't be changed, because it has already happened. The future can't be changed because you can't change something that hasn't happened any more than you can change something that has. I have to 'accept the things I cannot change' and so do you.

"The courage to change the things I can'. Ok, what can I change? The answer... Me! And I can only change me, when? The answer.... Now, today. Not yesterday, not tomorrow. Me, today, that is it. You and I have traveled quite the journey to make it to this point. A lot of what I have shared with you is based on going from Powerless To Powerful understanding the 3 P's, Purpose, Possibility and Potential, using the concept of Positive Results come from being deliberate in Positive Thoughts and Positive Actions. The courage to become the best version of me comes from progress in the process. Progress today means I start today a little closer to the man I aspire to be because I am building off what I did yesterday. I cannot change yesterday, but I can alter tomorrow's course by the choices I make or don't make today.

Learning to live in a world where we set goals for our future, it is tough sometimes, to learn to live in the present moment. My goals only happen if I put together progressive present moment thoughts and actions. One day a time is a big deal when you learn to live that way. The vision for this book and its completion only happens because I take present moment thoughts and actions using experiences of my past and record them one letter, one word at a time until it is complete.

Accomplishing anything worthwhile is like sitting down at a table and putting together a puzzle. You've put together a puzzle, right? What if the puzzle in front of you was a puzzle called life. I bet you would be like most men, sitting frantically trying to put it together being convinced you are missing most of the pieces. Anger, frustration, disappointment, fill in the blank, I have been there. If this puzzle is called my life, I want it to be finished, because when I get all the pieces in place, I will finally be happy.

The Puzzle Called Life is actually a training in *The P2PThirty Program*. The short version is that as we men try frantically to put this puzzle together, what we need is someone to tap us on the shoulder and ask us a question. "Have you turned the top of the box over to see what the picture looks like?" When I do, all kinds of magic happens. But, here is the point of the training... The picture on the top of My Puzzle Called Life, better be one I have deliberately painted for myself. God wants me to be the co-creator of my life. He puts in me purpose, possibility and potential, but I have to have a vision. Men without vision are lost. Men without vision get bored with life if their present day is putting together a puzzle they feel like they are forced to put together that someone else created.

Discover More About *The Puzzle Called Life* at; PowerlessToPowerfulTheBook.com

The Puzzle Called Life works when it is your picture, and you know that happiness is a present moment emotion based on your satisfaction with life as you, put the puzzle together a piece at a time, to create a life defined by passion and purpose.

I can't change the past, but I can begin today by making the future one of my own choosing, because I am becoming the best version of me I can. 'The wisdom to know the difference', is actually a prayer saying, "God, Thank You!"

Powerless To Powerful Chapter 22. The Phase 3 G. Grace

Grace is defined as 'the free and unmerited favor of God'. I just love that phrase and am going to say it again; 'the unmerited favor of God'. How many times have you heard someone say, "I am clean and sober today by the grace of God"? I know I have heard it said hundreds of times and I know, personally have used this phrase as it relates to how grateful I am for my time in recovery. Think about this for a moment; "I am clean and sober today by the unmerited favor of God." The purpose of this chapter is not to discount 'the grace of God', but to discuss how it relates to creating a life you are happy with on the positive side of addiction.

There are 2 sides to the principle of grace. There is God's side, which is the giving side. Then there is my side, which is the receiving side. Here's what I had to learn about this 'grace thing'. The unmerited favor of God is only as good as what I do to become willing to accept it.

There have been periods during my recovery where I required a little guidance to sort through my sometimes-chaotic level of thought. I learned early on, when I needed help, I had 2 choices; sit and be miserable, or ask for guidance. I was going through an extreme level of growth in my life, but I was struggling with what it meant. It was time for me to become better in several areas. I had begun going through Phase 3, The Discovery and Life's Purpose Phase and was looking at what my recovery meant and what God was calling me to do and to become. God put someone in my life to help me see the bigger picture, that at the time I was incapable of seeing alone. If you have seen the movie, *The Legend of Bagger Vance*, I was having one of those 'see the field' moments. If you haven't seen that movie, it is a must. It is one of the most powerful spiritual development movies disguised as an alcoholic playing golf. At that time in my life, God really spoke to me through that movie.

Remember back to the Phase 3 R, Relationships and The Power of The Mastermind. God works through people, and God at the time sure worked through a counselor I went to see. Peggy B. asked me in one of our sessions, "If I was to offer you a gift, are you willing to accept it?" My answer was, "Yes, but I can repay you and I can do this, and I can do that......" Peggy simply said, "No, that's not what I am asking you. If I am willing to offer you a gift, are you willing to accept it? Yes or No". I am certain that's where I began to learn about the unmerited favor of God. And as Bagger Vance said in the movie, I began to 'see the field'.

I was created in the image and likeness of God. That means I was born with unmerited favor. I get that. But, here's the question; "If I am born in the masculine image of God, what happens if I feel I am unworthy of that favor?" You have heard me say many times that my addictions had separated me from God. I went through a period in my active addiction where I didn't feel worthy of anything, especially the unmerited favor of God. I was on a roll making bad decisions because my addiction was my priority. It was doing everything to keep itself alive and it was winning. Here is what I have come to realize about that time. The unmerited favor of God was always there and available for me, I was just unwilling to see it and unwilling to take the actions to accept it. I had blinders on and the unmerited favor of God was a burning bush right next to me.

I saw a social media post the other day where a guy said, "10 years clean today by the grace of God." I congratulated him as I do with most people. I said something like, "A true example of what's possible". But I also said, "Be sure and give yourself credit as well. God did His part and will continue to do so. But, you have obviously done yours". That is what I had to understand about the unmerited favor of God; it wasn't worth much if I didn't act on it. God is not going to do this for me. The unmerited favor is God revealing the path. My part is my willingness to walk on that winding narrow path, accepting my God-given worthiness, building a powerful positive self-image. Are you beginning to see how many of the things we have talked about are connected? God puts us on this earth to help others 'connect the dots'.

I am clean and sober today by the grace of God, but I got a sponsor and worked the steps and went to meetings and chaired meetings and showed up early and stayed late. I have led aftercare groups and sponsored men and helped them through the steps. My path has led to me to the place where I create coaching programs and resources and write books to help men connect the dots. All of these things are available to me through the unmerited favor of God, but God didn't write this book. The music He put in my heart, but that music was mine to compose and sing.

My masculine soul, your masculine soul is offered to you through the unmerited favor of God. How do we accept this? Your acceptance, your part is in full view every single day in how you choose to live. Is life a drag, or is life an exciting adventure? Are you bored with your recovery or do you look for new ways to strengthen it? How are you in your love relationships? Do you treat the women in your life with God-given, God-inspired masculinity? Are you an example to other men of what a Powerful Godly man is? Does that show to your sons and daughters?

How much of this matters? ALL OF IT! The unmerited favor of God reveals itself in the way you and I live. If I don't accept it, and I am feeding the evil wolf. But, if I take the necessary actions, I am feeding the passionate purposeful wolf, that is an example of God working in me and through me. Think this is a huge challenge? HELL YES, IT IS! To dream huge and live huge in the creation and life's purpose phase of recovery is not for the timid. But, you and I are not timid. We are courageous and powerful by the unmerited favor of our Creator. The burning bush of grace is there, it is time for us to take off our blinders and act. The world needs Powerful Godly men. By God's grace and our actions, we reveal to the world the music God placed in our hearts.

Powerless To Powerful Chapter 23. The Phase 3 T2. Truth

I heard a guy giving away a chip at a meeting say something that at the time, my recovery ego took offense to. I know for me, there was an ego I had in active addiction, I had to work to put aside to live successfully in recovery. I also know that I had to build a recovery ego. This is, for a short time, a positive thing. Then I had to learn to let that go as well. Back to the meeting. This guy was giving away a 9-year chip and he was talking about the guy he was giving the chip to, when he said something that ruffled my feathers, shook my recovery ego a little. He said, "9 years is about when you start learning what the truth is." I was 6 years clean at the time and I thought, "He's crazy, I know what the truth is". Then, when it was time for me to celebrate my 9-year clean date, I can remember realizing, "You know, he was right".

My life in active addiction was a life defined by illusion. The insanity in the way I thought and the things I did kept me defending the illusion. It was a bad nightmare and I was convinced if everyone would just leave me alone, I would figure a way out. Yeah, right.

Our truth as human beings can be subjective to time and circumstance. For me, my journey to this point on the positive side of addiction has been a successful one. I have every reason, based on my experience, to hold that as my truth. The truth that going to treatment 1 time, remaining physically abstinent, getting a sponsor, working the steps and going to meetings works. This is my truth in Phase 1, The Physical Abstinence Phase. I have been around hundreds of other men that hold a completely different truth. They would say that this doesn't work, because they have tried it multiple times. Who is living in truth? I would say I am, and they are living in illusion. They would say something different

Most addicts and alcoholics would rather tell a lie, then to tell the truth, when the truth wouldn't hurt. No wonder we struggle with trust, right? So, how do we learn what is truth and what is not? Again, truth can be subjective. I know for me, I have learned a different level of truth in each of the 3 phases. Phase 1, I learn the truth about recovery. Phase 2, I learn the truth about myself. Phase 3 is where I learn the truth about God.

You and I have discussed the truth in Phase 1, right? I know my life improves when I remain physically abstinent from my addiction, one day at a time. In Phase 2, the truth is that in order to rebuild the life I crumbled because of my addiction, I had better apply, one day at a time to everything else. Phase 3 is my spiritual truth. This is where I develop a personal relationship with God that, for me, is bigger than meetings, bigger than my sponsor, bigger than church. "Oh no, Mark, don't go there!" Wait a minute. I didn't say instead of meetings and church, I said bigger than meetings and church.

In Phase 3, The Discovery and Life's Purpose Phase, God invites me to be the co-creator of my life with Him. Remember back to our conversation about 'Grace'? This is what I mean. The 'favor of God' is your invitation. Your powerful self-worth, should you choose to claim it and act on it is the 'favor of God'. Allow me to give you a little secret I learned. This is the truth of God I find in Phase 3. 'I can't do what God does and He won't do what I can'. Think about that for a minute.

Step 12 claims that I have had a 'spiritual awakening as a result of these steps'. If I don't find the truth that God invites me to co-create my life with Him, then I haven't had much of a spiritual awakening. If you limit this truth to just physical abstinence and a life of just barely miserable, but not really happy, there is so much more God has for you. If that's where you stop, and just hover, never going back, that's ok. But wouldn't it be a shame to leave something on the table? God has a storehouse full of abundance available to you. He has that for me and for every other person ever created. That is The Phase 3 Truth.

The truth as I know it.

- God created me in His image and likeness.
- I have a powerful masculine soul and a self-worth to match
- I have allowed my addiction to separate me from God
- My recovery is my personal responsibility
- I must live in the solution
- Recovery is one of the most powerful personal growth platforms
- When I accept my powerful self-worth, I will work on building a positive self-image
- Recovery erases my separation from God
- Being a Powerful Godly man is a daily decision
- When I do the right thing, it makes it easy to continue doing the right thing
- I must surround myself with people who think bigger than I do
- My enthusiasm for life shows God I am grateful
- True humility means accepting the powerful man God created me to be
- I must seek for what is right and true
- You will find God's will for you in the last chapter of this book.

Powerless To Powerful Chapter 24. The Phase 3 H. Happiness

Most men who have battled life in active addiction have built for themselves a prison. After they have been there for a while, they convince themselves that they are imprisoned there for life. Their ambitions, their self-image, a life of new possibilities and unlimited potential, held hostage. As soon as that belief wins, they seem to abandon any chance for the life they have dreamed about. They struggle and accept a life of mediocrity as their fate. They confine themselves and begin the process of accepting a living death. It is a rejection of the power and purpose given to them by their Creator. But, it doesn't have to remain that way. There is hope. They can walk away from the prison that defines living death and find the miracles available for them on the positive side of addiction.

"Mark, what makes you happy?" I remember the first time Finney C. asked me that question. Finney was another one of those 'right time, right place angels, God sent me on my journey. She was a counselor and a friend. She helped me realize several things. First being, that truth, like you and I discussed in the last chapter, was subjective to time. She helped me see that the day I checked into treatment was, for me at the time, the worst day of my life. Seeing my life as it is today, I can see that it was one of the best days. The next thing she helped me realize was that the quicker I dealt with the wreckage of my past, the quicker I could get on with the life that was waiting for me.

Back about 12 years ago, Finney's journey on this earth ended. At her visitation, I met her son, Todd. He asked me how I knew his mom. I told him that she was one of the people who God put in my life that helped change the course of my life forever. We chatted a few moments and he told me when I signed the book to put down how long I had been clean and sober, so he could remember our conversation. I did as he asked and wrote my name and 7 years. I didn't think much about it, wiped my eyes and left. A couple weeks later I get a small envelope in the mail. Inside the envelope is a couple pieces of cardboard and some recovery medallions taped to them and a handwritten note;

Mark, I hope this finds you well. Thank you for coming out to our mom's visitation; we thoroughly enjoyed meeting those who were important to her. Inside you will find Finney's 8, 9, 10 and 11-year medallions, which we want you to have if you like. I recommend you carry them only in due time. When you are done with them, simply recycle them at your home group or pass them on as you see fit.

How do I remember exactly what that card says? I can pick it up and read it. It meant that much to me. And yes, I carried those medallions in due time and recycled them as he asked. It was an honor. This to me is the real gift of God working through others. Finney blessed my life while she was alive and continued to do so even in her death.

Back to the question she asked me; "Mark, what makes you happy?" When I started this long-drawn-out answer, she quickly stopped me, because my answer for what made me happy was contingent on someone or something else. I sat there confused and dejected and said, 'Finney, I don't know. I don't know what makes me happy." Her response, "How can you expect to be in a relationship, how can you expect to have a career, how can you expect anyone else to bring you happiness, if you don't know what that means to you?"

You and I ended our last conversation and I made a bold declaration; You would find God's will for you in the final chapter. Well, here we are. Any man who has spent any time in recovery asks himself over and over; "What is God's will for me?" Then he'll make a statement, "I wish I could figure out God's will for me." Then it's, "Can anyone help me find God's will for me?" Well here it is. It comes from Lessons 101 and 102 in A Course In Miracles;

101: God's Will For Me Is Perfect Happiness

102: I Share God's Will For Happiness For Me

I have studied A Course in Miracles several different times in the last decade, but I will never forget the way I felt the first time I read that. It's still the way I feel today as I share it with you. I said, "YES! I GET IT NOW!" I was so grateful that I didn't have to figure out God's will, but I had to define what happiness meant to me. Back to Finney's question, "Mark, what makes you happy?"

Happiness is like truth, it is subjective. It has different meanings for different men. Things that bring me joy and happiness in my life may not do it for you. I got sick of hearing, 'happiness is a journey, not a destination'. Ok, great. What does that mean? I hear that, and I'm still confused. So, I came up with a definition of what Ashley and I call, The Happiness Principle. The Happiness Principle states that;

Happiness is a present moment emotion that is based on #1 making peace with my past, #2 taking actions in my present, toward #3 a vision I have for my future.

In Phase 1, I worked the steps and was able to make peace with my past. In Phase 2, I continued that process and learned that actions in the present moment, this one day at a time thing, worked on everything else. And finally, in Phase 3, I discovered that God's will for me and my will for me were the same; To live a happy and passionate life. For that very reason, I learned that my future was one that I can co-create with God. I discovered the purpose for my recovery and awakened my unlimited potential to discover the purpose for my life.

Happiness is not some elusive, out there somewhere that I have no idea what it is or looks like. Happiness is peace in the present moment and hope for my future. My happiness isn't contingent on any 1 thing or any person. Happiness is a choice. It is a way of living. Ahhhhh, now I understand the 'journey thing'. God's will for me is to make peace with my past and take actions in the present to co-create my life with Him.

So, what is God's will for you? His will for you is your will for you, right? God's will for you is my will for you; Perfect Happiness.

We have come to the end of our journey into The Great Awakening of The Masculine Soul. I hope you have enjoyed this fireside chat. I know I have. My goal again, as I said when we first started was to share my experience and strength, and by the time we made it to here, you would say, "Yeah, This Is The Way I Really Want To Think, Too!"

My hope for you is this:

- If there was something you were looking for and haven't found, I got you a little closer.
- If what brought you here was boredom and complacency with your life and your recovery, that this awakened a passion in you.
- If you are confused, I connected some dots and shortened your learning curve.
- If you haven't found God working through others yet, that you are willing to keep looking.
- That you are ready to celebrate your uniqueness and discover your strengths to be of maximum service to others.
- That from this day forward, you will choose to be a Powerful God-ly man and be an example to the world, unapologetically, of what true God-given, God-inspired masculinity looks and feels like.
- That when you are ready, and this is a tough one, because God knows you're ready long before you do, that you allow Him to help you become a man of impact and go from Powerless To Powerful.

For More, Go To: PowerlessToPowerfulTheBook.com

Meet Mark and Ashley.

In 1999, Mark Mascolo, checked into a drug and alcohol rehabilitation center in Nashville, Tn. He was a husband, a father, and a business owner. Through a series of unfortunate decisions, his Amer-  ican Dream was becoming a nightmare. He found his company, his marriage and his life falling apart. As a successful college athlete, Mark had always been a 'give me the ball, let's do this thing' kind of guy. But this addiction thing had gotten too big. He needed some help.

In 2000, a successful banker and commercial lender, Ashley DePriest, checked herself into the same treatment facility. Ashley's life in the rat race had her asking questions about her future that had her settling for far less than she wanted. Living a life most people would dream of, she was coming apart inside. Her marriage was unraveling as was her physical health. She made a decision. She told herself, "I don't care what I do, I just can't do this anymore."

Enter a lot of Divine Intervention. God had a plan and a purpose much greater than these 2 could have ever imagined. When they met, they had no idea what God had in store. As with most endings, men and women of faith believe in new beginnings. Mark and Ashley began their life together. With Mark's creative and passionate entrepreneurial spirit and Ashley's master level studies in psychology and her business background, they found themselves looking to serve a higher purpose than the careers that had led them both to addiction.

God's purpose became their purpose. Together, Mark and Ashley through their passion for personal and professional growth and accelerated human performance, backed by more than 36 years of combined study, are experts in the little-known, but ever-expanding field of Positive Psychology. They are passionate about sharing God's message of purpose, possibility and potential through the products, programs and events they create. 2 Broken Roads, 1 Direction, God's Plan, 1 Purpose.

To Find Out More or To Contact Mark and Ashley

PowerlessToPowerfulTheBook.com